TRUSTING
IN THE
NAMES
OF GOD

TRUSTING IN THE NAMES OF GOD

CATHERINE MARTIN

HARVEST HOUSE PUBLISHERS

EUGENE, OREGON

Catherine Martin: Published in association with the literary agency of WordServe Literary Group, Ltd., 10152 S. Knoll Circle, Highlands Ranch, CO 80130.

Cover by Koechel Peterson & Associates, Inc., Minneapolis, Minnesota

Cover photo © Photos.com

TRUSTING IN THE NAMES OF GOD
Copyright © 2008 by Catherine Martin
Published by Harvest House Publishers
Eugene, Oregon 97402
www.harvesthousepublishers.com

Library of Congress Cataloging-in-Publication Data

Martin, Catherine, 1956-
    Trusting in the names of God / Catherine Martin.
        p.cm.
    ISBN-13: 978-0-7369-2345-3
    ISBN-10: 0-7369-2345-4
    1. God—Name—Biblical teaching. 2. Trust in God. 3. Devotional exercises. I. Title.
BT180.N2M375 2008
231—dc22

2007052790

Dedicated to Dr. Ronald Youngblood, chairman of the board of directors of International Bible Society and Professor Emeritus of Old Testament and Hebrew at Bethel Theological Seminary in San Diego. Dr. Youngblood is a translator of the NIV and a member of the Committee for Bible Translation for the NIV and TNIV.

Thank you, Dr. Youngblood, for teaching me to study God's Word with diligence, joyfully write books with dedication, serve God with faithfulness, and love the Lord with all my heart. Thank you for being one of my great examples in life and a hero of the faith.

And those who know Your name will put their trust in You.
Psalm 9:10

Who is among you that fears the LORD,
that obeys the voice of His servant,
that walks in darkness and has no light?
Let him trust in the name of the LORD
and rely on his God.
Isaiah 50:10

Some trust in chariots and some in horses,
but we trust in the name of the LORD our God.
Psalm 20:7 NIV

CONTENTS

Foreword 9

Introduction 13

Week One: Knowing God's Names

Day 1: The Great Adventure of Knowing God 23

Day 2: God Has Revealed Himself to You 31

Day 3: You Can Know His Names 37

Day 4: Responding to the Names of God 43

Day 5: How to Trust in the Names of God 49

Day 6: Quiet Time Week One: Knowing God's Names 55

Week Two: Trusting in God's Names

Day 7: Discover His Names 63

Day 8: Draw Near to His Names 71

Day 9: Declare His Names 79

Day 10: Depend on His Names 85

Day 11: Delight in His Names 93

Day 12: Quiet Time Week Two: Trusting in God's Names 99

Week Three: Discovering God's Greatness and Glory

Day 13: Trusting in Elohim—He Is Your Creator 107

Day 14: Trusting in El Elyon—He Is Your Sovereign 115

Day 15: Trusting in Adonai—He Is Your Lord 123

Day 16: Trusting in El Shaddai—He Is Enough for You 131

Day 17: Trusting in Yahweh Jireh—He Is Your Provider 139

Day 18: Quiet Time Week Three: Trusting God As Abraham Did 149

Week Four: Discovering God's Person and Presence

Day 19: Trusting in El Roi—He Sees You 155

Day 20: Trusting in Yahweh—He Is Everything You Need 163

Day 21: Trusting in Yahweh Rophe—He Is Your Healer. 173

Day 22: Trusting in Yahweh Nissi—He Is Your Victory 179

Day 23: Trusting in Yahweh Mekaddesh—He Makes You Holy 187

Day 24: Quiet Time Week Four: Trusting God As Moses Did 195

Week Five: Discovering God's Care and Concern

Day 25: Trusting in Yahweh Shalom—He Is Your Peace. 203

Day 26: Trusting in Yahweh Sabaoth—He Is Your Deliverer 211

Day 27: Trusting in Yahweh Ro'i—He Is Your Shepherd 219

Day 28: Trusting in Abba, Father—He Is Your Father 227

Day 29: To God Be the Glory. 237

Day 30: Quiet Time Week Five: Trusting God As David Did 241

Appendix 1: Discussion Questions 249

Appendix 2: More Tools for Trusting in the Names of God 261

Notes. 271

FOREWORD

We often form an opinion of people the first time we meet them. That was surely the case when I first met Catherine Martin 20 years ago. She had matriculated at Bethel Seminary San Diego and had enrolled in one of my courses. Although the class was large—it was required of all entering students—she stood out from the rest primarily because of her glowing smile. Always cheerful and lively, she reminded me a bit of Katie Couric. Come to think of it, I can't ever remember seeing Catherine when she didn't have a smile on her face.

As it turned out, she had much more than just a bubbly personality. She quickly demonstrated the diligent and systematically determined side of her nature as she waltzed through all three of my courses in which she had enrolled. Those who know Catherine will not be surprised to learn that she earned an A in each of them—effortlessly, as nearly as I could gauge. It soon became clear that she was an exceptional student, concluding her formal education at Bethel with a 4.0 GPA and graduating summa cum laude with a master of arts degree in theological studies.

Catherine's ministry in the service of Christ began long before she came to Bethel. She had worked for Josh McDowell and Bill Bright for several years, and she served as a women's Bible-study leader for more than a decade, including during her time as a seminary student. It was only natural, then, that she should found and direct an organization such as Quiet Time Ministries soon after graduation.

Growing up in Chicago as a young Christian, I was advised by my spiritual mentors to spend a quiet time every day with my Lord. That meant that I was to read my Bible and pray every day—a worthy and important spiritual exercise. Some years ago I discovered that the phrases "quiet time" and "Catherine Martin" are virtual synonyms—or at least they are closely associated with each other in the minds of many people. I typed "quiet time" into Google and instantly gained access to more than two million references to that phrase. The third reference on the first page was about

Catherine Martin's Quiet Time Ministries. She is obviously making a deep and lasting spiritual impact on a wide audience of Bible readers and prayer partners throughout the United States and beyond.

And *Trusting in the Names of God* will doubtless extend that impact. Choosing many of the most significant Hebrew names of God found in the Old Testament, she tells her readers why they should place their trust— with whole-soul devotion—in *El Shaddai* ("God Almighty"), *El Roi* ("The God Who Sees Me"), *El Elyon* ("God Most High"), *Yahweh* (the Lord, the great "I AM"), *Yahweh Shalom* ("The Lord is Peace"), *Yahweh Nissi* ("The Lord Is My Banner"), *Yahweh Ro'i* ("The Lord Is My Shepherd"), and on and on. She also makes it clear that the many names do not denote many gods but are all names of the one true God, our Creator and Redeemer, the Father, who sent His Son to be the Savior of the world. A name in ancient Israel was not simply a tag or a title but also referred to a person's essence, character, and personality. Therefore, to trust in God's names, to love God's names, to delight in God's names meant to trust, to love, to delight in God Himself. For this reason, if for no other, Catherine Martin's *Trusting in the Names of God* will inspire you and will strengthen your walk with Jesus, to whom all of the names of our God in the Old Testament ultimately point.

Ronald Youngblood
Emeritus Professor of Old Testament
Bethel Seminary San Diego

A Prayer of Trust

Lord, I would trust Thee completely;
I would be altogether Thine; I would exalt Thee above all.
I desire that I may feel no sense of possessing anything outside of Thee.
I want constantly to be aware of Thy overshadowing Presence
and to hear Thy speaking Voice.
I long to live in restful sincerity of heart.
I want to live so fully in the Spirit
that all my thoughts may be as sweet incense ascending to Thee
and every act of my life may be an act of worship.
Therefore I pray in the words of Thy great servant of old,
"I beseech Thee so for to cleanse the intent of mine heart
with the unspeakable gift of Thy grace,
that I may perfectly love Thee and worthily praise Thee."
And all this I confidently believe Thou wilt grant me
through the merits of Jesus Christ Thy Son.
Amen.

A.W. Tozer

INTRODUCTION

Every person is given a life span by Almighty God. Moses exclaimed, "So teach us to number our days, that we may present to you a heart of wisdom" (Psalm 90:12). Billy Graham explains, "Our days are numbered…the legacy we leave is…in the quality of our lives." A.W. Tozer exhorts, "Refuse to be average. Let your heart soar as high as it will." So, my friend, dear reader, the question I ask of you is, "How will you spend the days of your life?"

I think of Charles Spurgeon, who lived merely 58 years and yet wrote more than 3000 sermons, many books, and countless articles. Robert Murray McCheyne lived only 29 years, but the story of his intimate relationship with God in *Memoirs of McCheyne* has impacted thousands. Henry Scougal's *The Life of God in the Soul of Man,* written for a friend but read by generations, has influenced uncounted lives, and he only lived 27 years on earth. Although Oswald Chambers died in 1917 at the age of 43, his book *My Utmost for His Highest* continues to be a bestseller.

What is the secret of such influence and accomplishment? Very simply, these men knew their God, they experienced Him firsthand in their lives, and they ventured to tell others about their discoveries. Do you know God? Have you discovered who He is, what He does, and what He says? Do you know what delights Him? Do you know what breaks His heart? If your answer to these questions is yes, you are on the path to a life well spent in the things that matter most and last forever. You are, as Jesus encouraged us, laying up treasure in heaven (Matthew 6:20).

Early in my life, I made the decision to lay aside the "many things" for the "one thing." This decision did not come about in a haphazard manner or as the result of a lightning bolt from heaven, but as a direct result of the diligent study of the Word of God. One day, I was deep into a reference Bible study leading me through Psalms, and I arrived at Psalm 27:4. I read these words: "One thing I have asked from the LORD, that I shall seek: that I may dwell in the house of the LORD all the days of my life, to behold the beauty of the LORD and to meditate in His temple." The words *one thing* leaped off the page, grabbed my heart, and occupied the forefront of my mind for days on end. The meaning was self-evident. I must be single-minded and single-hearted in my pursuit of God Himself.

Two books in particular greatly influenced me during that time of meditation and contemplation: *Knowing God* by J.I. Packer and *The Pursuit of God* by A.W. Tozer. I speak of these books often in my lectures, messages, and books because I respect the authors' profound articulation of what it means to know God. After reading Packer and Tozer, I became passionate about knowing God. I wanted the experience of knowing Him. I didn't want merely to talk *about* God. I didn't want only to talk *to* God. I wanted to talk *with* God. I wanted to walk *with* God. I wanted to know Him, not as I thought He should be but as He really is. That was my decision.

We have before us a great opportunity for knowing God. Are we content to settle for talking about God, or will we set aside the many things for the one thing, draw near, and know Him for ourselves? I recently received an e-mail from a friend that touched me deeply. In it he said, "Include me in your prayers please—I've been making a slow turn back toward faith in Christ after 15 years of agnosticism...personal relationship with God/Christ is still an incredible mystery to me in any kind of experiential sense."

My friend is further along in his journey with God than a lot of people. For many in the church today, knowing and loving God is a mystery with very little seen or sought in firsthand experience. This is similar to the period prior to the Reformation. How do I know this? More than 50 percent of churchgoers never open their Bibles outside of their time in church. This tells me that the church is full of observers rather than participants. That may sound like harsh commentary to some, but I make this observation because I am greatly burdened to see those who are thirsty find the abundant water that is available to quench the deepest desires in the hearts of men and women.

God promises, "You will seek Me and find Me when you search for Me with all your heart" (Jeremiah 29:13). He invites you to the greatest adventure of all: "Cease striving and know that I am God" (Psalm 46:10). God made our hearts in such a way that only He satisfies our deepest desires. He said to Abraham, "I am your shield, your very great reward" (Genesis 15:1 NIV).

The answer for the church today is not new angles, new strategies, or new programs, but Spirit-taught knowledge of God discovered in well-worn Bibles that are studied and read by all. There is no substitution for Spirit-filled work in the heart of a person when God opens up His Word and gives a golden nugget of truth. Thousands of such nuggets are awaiting your discovery. God meets you through His Word in the circumstances of your life. That, my friend, is when life moves from a journey to an adventure!

When you jump into the adventure of knowing God, disappointments become God's appointments. I remember when God showed me a new truth about Himself from Ephesians 3:20-21 and Isaiah 55:9. Years ago, long before my seminary days, I decided to have a Bible study in my home in San Diego in answer to the deep desire in my heart to teach and study the Word of God with others. So I sent out the invitations and prayed. On the day of the study I rose early, prepared the coffee, and set up the room, laying out the books in perfect arrangement on my dining room table. As the time approached for the study to begin, I nervously paced back and forth from the dining room to the front door. Time was passing, and no one had arrived. Finally, the time was past for the study to begin. As the reality settled in, I fell to the floor sobbing, brokenhearted that no one had shown up for my Bible study.

I called my friend Judy and told her the sad news. She prayed with me on the telephone. I was so discouraged with the thought that I would never get to lead a Bible study or teach the Bible. Then I remembered what I learned about God from Ephesians—that He "is able to do immeasurably more than all we ask or imagine" (Ephesians 3:20), and His ways are higher than my ways (Isaiah 55:9). *Hmm…*I pondered, wiping away the tears, *I wonder what that means for me on a day when no one has come to my Bible study?* Well, later that day I found out! I received a phone call from my church telling me about a group that had lost their Bible study leader. They were calling to ask me if I would consider moving my Bible study to the church. Of course I said yes, and when I walked into the room the first night, I found 25 men and women waiting to learn about God and study the Bible! Through that experience, God began to teach me to trust what He says, who He is, and what He does more than how I feel about my circumstances in my life. God has a plan and longs to carry out that plan through people who will walk by faith in devotion to Him.

And that is why I have written this book. I want you to trust who God is more than how you feel or what you see happening in the circumstances of your life. This book is for hungry hearts that are unwilling to settle for a travelogue on God. No longer content with crumbs, you desire a feast from God in His Word and want to know Him deeply.

Knowing God will alter the course of your life. Knowing God will change how you live, influence the decisions you make, and shape your responses to trials and adverse circumstances. Knowing God changes the books you read and designs your circle of friends. Knowing God leads you into daily divine appointments. When you know God, you will learn to trust God rather than trusting people, money, and possessions. Jeremiah learned the great value of trusting God: "Blessed are those who trust in the LORD, whose confidence is in him. He will be like a tree planted by the water that sends out its roots by the stream. It does not fear when the heat comes; its leaves are always green. It has no worries in a year of drought and never fails to bear fruit" (Jeremiah 17:7-8). As you know God, you will, like Jeremiah, learn the great value of trusting Him.

If you are going to engage in the pursuit of knowing God, how can you do it? How can you trust one whom you do not know? Very simply, through knowing and trusting His names. God doesn't have just one name, but many names. Through His names, He has revealed His character—who He is, what He does, and what He says. *Trusting in the Names of God* is a journey into the heart of God. We will spend 30 days contemplating the unfathomable one who loves us and who, through His names, has shown us He desires an intimate relationship with us.

How to Use *Trusting in the Names of God*

Each week you will *read, respond,* and *experience:*

Read. In each day's reading, interact with the ideas by underlining what is significant to you and writing your comments in the margins. This book will encourage you to learn who God is, grow in your relationship with Him, and develop a great trust in Him. Please mark it up and make it yours! You will also want to keep your Bible close by to look up those verses that mean the most to you on this 30-day journey.

Respond. To help you think through and apply all that is written here, I have included a devotional response section at the end of each day. You'll find a key verse for you to meditate on and memorize, questions to consider, and a place to express your thoughts and respond to what you have read. This is your opportunity to dialogue with God about who He is and your growing relationship with Him. (Appendix 2 includes a worksheet where you can write out each name of God and its meaning during this 30-day journey.)

Experience. A complete quiet time at the end of every week emphasizes the principles in that section. Use the blank Notes page to record what you learn from the *Trusting in the Names of God* companion DVD.

Share your journey. Read what others are learning on their journey through *Trusting in the Names of God* and share your own insights with others throughout the world by posting your thoughts on the Quiet Time Ministries discussion board at www.quiettimecafe.com.

Suggested Approaches

You can benefit from this book in several ways:

Sequentially. You may want to read the book a day at a time and implement the principles before moving to the next chapter.

Topically. You may have specific topics of interest to you. If that is the case, you can look at the table of contents and focus on those topics.

Devotionally. You may choose to read this book over 30 days. The days are divided into five sections so you can take five weeks to read and think about the names of God. It can be a 30-day adventure!

SUGGESTED SETTINGS

Personal and private. This is the kind of book you can read again and again. It will encourage you to draw near to God, especially if you have lost a habit of time with your Lord in His Word or you need to shake up your quiet time because it has become lackluster and routine. You might even want to spend some extended time with this book in a beautiful setting to revive and refresh your relationship with the Lord. It's a retreat in a book!

Small groups. I encourage you to travel on this 30-day journey with some friends. Sharing what you are learning with others who also love the Lord brings tremendous joy. Use the questions at the end of each day for your discussion together. More discussion questions are in appendix 1. This book may be used in Sunday school classes, Bible study groups, church congregations, or your family devotions.

Ministry spiritual growth campaign. You may also desire to use this book as a 30-day intensive campaign to teach, revive, and inspire those in your ministry in the area of knowing and trusting God. Using it as a campaign will help grow your ministry as new small groups are formed. For more information about how to use his book as a spiritual growth campaign for your group, visit these websites:

www.30dayjourney.com
www.trustinginthenamesofgod.com

COMPANION RESOURCES

- The *Quiet Time Notebook* and Devotional Bible Study pages

- *Trusting in the Names of God Journal*

- *Trusting in the Names of God DVD*

- *Trusting in the Names of God—A Quiet Time Experience* (Harvest House, 2008) is an eight-week devotional Bible study in quiet-time format according to the P.R.A.Y.E.R. plan introduced in *Six Secrets to a Powerful Quiet Time* (Harvest House, 2005).

- *Trusting in the Names of God* bookmark. Download free at www.quiettime.org.

Now let's set out on this great adventure of knowing God! I am so excited to walk with you in the great corridors of Scripture, where God reveals Himself in His names. We are going to venture into some of the magnificent rooms in the Bible, where even a single verse opens up a whole new world. Dear friend, leave your cares at the door, grab your Bible, and let's launch out on this exciting journey into the wonder and majesty of God Himself.

The Thought of God

The thought of God, the thought of Thee,
Who liest in my heart,
And yet beyond imagined space
Outstretched and present art—
The thought of Thee, above, below,
Around me and within,
Is more to me than health and wealth,
Or love of kith and kin.
The thought of God is like the tree
Beneath whose shade I lie,
And watch the fleets of snowy clouds
Sail o'er the silent sky.
'Tis like that soft invading light,
Which in all darkness shines,
The thread that through life's somber web
In golden pattern twines.
It is a thought which ever makes
Life's sweetest smiles from tears,
And is a daybreak to our hopes,
A sunset to our fears.
One while it bids the tears to flow,
Then wipes them from the eyes,
Most often fills our souls with joy,
And always sanctifies.
Within a thought so great, our souls
Little and modest grow,
And, by its vastness awed we learn
The art of walking slow.[1]

FREDERICK WILLIAM FABER

Week One

KNOWING
GOD'S NAMES

Days 1–6

Day One

THE GREAT ADVENTURE
OF KNOWING GOD

*Thus says the LORD, "Let not a wise man boast of his wisdom,
and let not the mighty man boast of his might, let not a rich
man boast of his riches; but let him who boasts boast of this,
that he understands and knows Me, that I am the LORD
who exercises lovingkindness, justice and righteousness on
earth; for I delight in these things," declares the LORD.*

JEREMIAH 9:23-24

The greatest claim you can make in your life is that you know God. No greater ambition or endeavor can match the intimacy you enjoy with God during a brief stay on earth and in full measure in eternity. The Lord, in fact, says that He delights in the person who understands and knows Him. He says, "Let him who boasts boast that he understands and knows Me, that I am the LORD who exercises lovingkindness, justice and righteousness on earth; for I delight in these things" (Jeremiah 9:24). The Hebrew word *yada,* translated "know," means intimate knowledge, implying a firsthand experience with the one who is known.

To be able to say "I have known God" counts more than saying "I have made a million dollars" or "I have a doctoral degree." To be sure, those accomplishments are of worth, but only in small degree compared to the eternal value of knowing God. And so, somewhere along the way in life, a person must come to a decision about how to spend his or her life.

One summer my husband and I traveled to Paris for two weeks. We soon discovered that we had not chosen the ideal time of year for our trip. The weather was so stifling hot that we spent two hours one evening simply searching for a restaurant with air conditioning. Hungry and fatigued, we walked down the Champs Elysées toward the Place de la Concorde, popping our heads in and out of restaurants and hotels to no avail. Our searching seemed at a dead end. Just as we were about to give up, we happened on Le Meurice, a hotel across from the Tuileries Gardens. We passed through the grand lobby and entered the most wonderful restaurant we had ever seen—Louis XVI style with antique mirrors, crystal chandeliers, a ceiling fresco of angels…and air conditioning. We were thrilled at our discovery. My husband and I spent hours relishing the food and lingering over intimate conversation. We often speak of our delightful Paris adventure.

Knowing God is like our journey in Paris—a great adventure with unexpected surprises and discoveries. I discovered early on that God delights to teach me His Word and bids me to trust and wait on Him. Then, He applies the truth of His Word to my life in sometimes straightforward and sometimes unusual ways.

In my early years as a new Christian, I focused on learning about God as I read and studied the Bible. I sought out books on His character and attributes and wrote down everything I learned about God in my journal. I truly wanted to know what He was like; I wanted to know Him. I read the Bible with the scrutiny and delight that one would give to a love letter.

Perhaps my most important discovery was that God loved me. I read many verses about God's love for me. "For God so loved the world, that He gave His only begotten Son, that whoever believes in Him shall not perish, but have eternal life" (John 3:16). This well-loved and famous verse taught me that God's love was sacrificial and demonstrative. Then I read in 1 John 4:9 that God is the one who initiates our love relationship: "In this is love, not that we loved God, but that He loved us and sent His Son to be the propitiation for our sins." I discovered that God's love for me is "an everlasting love" (Jeremiah 31:3) and can be comprehended in breadth, length, height, and depth (Ephesians 3:18).

In those early years, I also discovered that applying what I was learning about God's love was quite a challenge. It so happened that my friend Helen and I were given the opportunity to attend a concert of one of my favorite gospel artists at the time, Evie Tornquist. I had all her albums and knew the words to every one of her songs. I asked my employer if I could take the evening off from work to attend the concert. But much to my dismay, she denied my request. I was absolutely stunned and fell into despair. More than anything I wanted to hear Evie sing.

Helen told me that if I couldn't go to the concert, she wasn't going to go either. Her response shocked me. I couldn't imagine that she would give up her opportunity out of love for me. What a demonstration of the love of God I learned from Helen and her action on my behalf. At the time, I probably would not have done the same.

The night of the concert, after work, I remember going home, running to my room, and throwing myself on my bed, disheartened at the lost opportunity to hear Evie. As I lay there in bed with my head buried facedown in my pillow, I heard the words of Jeremiah 31:3 whispered in my mind: "I have loved you with an everlasting love." I lifted my head off the pillow. I thought, *Can God's love endure, and can He express His love in my life even in spite of great disappointment and loss?* I thought about Jeremiah's words, and I realized that everlasting love goes on forever. It never ends—it endures every hardship, every trial, every loss. God will express His everlasting love for me in His own spectacular way and in His own perfect time. The power of the truth I learned that night about His love has carried me through much heartache and many more difficult trials to this day.

Many years later I did attend an Evie concert, and I smile at the bitter disappointment I felt over something so trivial compared to much greater losses I've experienced since that time. I also smile because God has given me such incredible opportunities and unbelievable expressions of His love, far surpassing a simple one-night concert. I have learned not to define how God can and should work in my life. Knowing God is the great adventure because He delights in expressing who He is in our lives. We see this delight in His proclamation to Moses when He passed by, declaring, "The LORD, the LORD God, compassionate and gracious, slow to anger, and abounding in lovingkindness and truth; who keeps lovingkindness for thousands, who forgives iniquity, trangression and sin" (Exodus 34:6-7).

When I lived in Dallas and was involved in the Josh McDowell Ministry, I meditated on the Great Commission in Matthew 28:18-20. Reading these verses moved me to pray that God would give me a new and deeper vision for the world. I wanted to move beyond my own limited view of Dallas, where I lived, and Phoenix, where I had grown up. I thought maybe the Lord would answer my prayer by taking me on a journey to Africa or New Guinea or who knew where.

One morning not too long after that prayer, I was reading the Dallas paper. An advertisement caught my eye promoting the World Gymnastics Championships in Fort Worth, about an hour from Dallas. I was excited to read this ad because when I was a little girl I was a gymnast and had dreamed of one day being part of the Olympics. When I was ten I was part of a gymnastic group called the Flamettes, performing back handsprings and backflips for audiences throughout Arizona.

I immediately determined I would attend the championships, bought a ticket, and arranged to travel to Fort Worth. Oh, I could not wait to get there. My heart pounded as I entered the arena. I saw the familiar mats, the balance beam, horse, and uneven parallel bars. I found my seat and was mesmerized with everything that was happening.

The lady sitting next to me could not believe how excited I was. She asked me why I was so excited. I told her about my gymnastics training, childhood aspirations, and my love for the sport. Then she told me how she had been able to attend the championships. Her husband was a security guard for the gymnasts and had been given free tickets. Then she said, "Catherine, how would you like to go backstage after the championships, eat dinner, and meet all the gymnasts?"

I could not believe I was hearing her invitation. I said, "That would be amazing. I would love to do that!"

After the event, she led me through a maze of chairs to a guarded door. She showed her pass, and we entered a huge room. What I saw took my breath away. All the gymnasts were sitting at tables marked by the flag of their country. After we had eaten, I excused myself and sauntered around the room, absorbing the atmosphere. I walked from section to section, observing all the talented gymnasts.

When I reached the gymnasts from the Eastern European countries, I looked into their eyes and saw an indescribable emptiness. Hollow. A love and compassion welled up in my heart for these gymnasts still behind the Iron Curtain. As I stood there, I wanted more than anything to tell them about Jesus and His love for them.

As I drove back to Dallas, I was confronted by so many urgent thoughts racing through my mind. How could I reach those girls with the message, the good news of Jesus? I hadn't quite realized there were so many people in the world. I hadn't considered that there were so many disparate places to live. I couldn't imagine that some people didn't have the same opportunities I had. It was difficult to believe that to some, the Bible was a closed book. I was sobered by what I had seen. I could not forget all the flags, all the countries, and all those girls.

Then I remembered my prayer, *Lord, give me a vision for the world.* How personal God is, to custom design an answer to that prayer. Only the God of the universe could use my gymnastics background, move me to Dallas on staff with Campus Crusade, bring the World Gymnastics Championship my way, place my seat next to the security guard's wife, and get me backstage to see the world. But that's what God does. And that's why I call knowing Him a great adventure. Only He can do "God things." And the ordinary becomes extraordinary because He is at work.

Friend, are you presently engaging in the great adventure of knowing God? How are you spending your life? Have you set aside the many things for the one thing—knowing Him? God extends an invitation to all of us:

> Come, all you who are thirsty, come to the waters; and you who have no money, come, buy and eat...why spend money on what is not bread, and your labor on what does not satisfy? Listen, listen to me and eat what is good, and you will delight in the richest of fare. Give ear and come to me; listen, that you may live...Seek the LORD while he may be found; call on him while he is near (Isaiah 55:1-3,6 TNIV).

Whether you are a pastor, missionary, laborer in the field, secretary in an office, or CEO of a large corporation, your highest and greatest aspiration should be knowing God and trusting in His names. Charles Spurgeon, the great nineteenth-century English preacher, speaking about the immutability of God, invited his listeners to make knowing God their great focus:

> Would you lose your sorrows? Would you drown your cares? Then go plunge yourself in the Godhead's deepest sea; be lost in His immensity; and you shall come forth as from a couch of rest, refreshed and invigorated. I know nothing which can so comfort the soul, so calm the swelling billows of grief and sorrow; so speak peace to the winds of trial, as a devout musing upon the subject of the Godhead.[1]

The things of earth can sometimes lead you to forgetfulness of this one great ambition in life. Remembering God and drawing near to Him is your great boast and what delights God. Many great men and women have known God. And you can join their great company and follow in their train—you may know Him too.

> Open my eyes, that I may see
> Glimpses of truth Thou hast for me;
> Place in my hands the wonderful key
> That shall unclasp and set me free.
> Silently now I wait for Thee;
> Ready, my God, Thy will to see,
> Open my eyes, illumine me,
> Spirit divine.

CLARA H. SCOTT

My Response

DATE:

KEY VERSE: "Thus says the LORD, 'Let not a wise man boast of his wisdom, and let not the mighty man boast of his might, let not a rich man boast of his riches; but let him who boasts boast of this, that he understands and knows Me, that I am the LORD who exercises lovingkindness, justice and righteousness on earth; for I delight in these things,' declares the LORD" (Jeremiah 9:23-24).

FOR FURTHER THOUGHT: As you begin this 30-day journey, take some time now to talk with the Lord about where you are in your relationship with Him and what you hope to gain from your time with Him in *Trusting in the Names of God*. Write a prayer to Him in the form of a letter in the space provided and then watch what He does in your life over the next 30 days.

MY RESPONSE: A Letter to the Lord

GOD HAS REVEALED HIMSELF TO YOU

*That which is known about God is evident within them;
for God made it evident to them. For since the creation
of the world His invisible attributes, His eternal power and
divine nature, have been clearly seen, being understood through
what has been made, so that they are without excuse.*

ROMANS 1:19-20

God may be known because He has chosen to make Himself known. You cannot discover anything about God except for what He has revealed. The amazing truth is that He has actually revealed Himself by declaring His names, His character, His works, and His ways. Can you imagine a human being bending down to ground level to reveal anything to an ant? Any illustration of the ways of God will be inadequate, but this picture still makes the point.

God's revelation of Himself to those He has created shows us we have an incomparable, compassionate, loving God, who is more than we know Him to be right now. He has chosen to take what many have called "the divine initiative," initiating a true relationship with us by revealing Himself to us. His revelation includes a *general* expression in creation as well as a *special* expression in the Bible and in the incarnation, where God entered the human race and was "made in human likeness" (Philippians 2:7 NIV). Jesus, the second person of the Triune God, is "the radiance of His glory and the exact representation of His nature" (Hebrews 11:3).

This expression is known as *revelation.* The word translated *revelation,* from the Greek *apokalypsis,* points to a disclosure or unveiling, signifying God unveiling Himself to mankind.[1] God's revelation is not without purpose—He desires an intimate relationship with us. In fact, in Romans 1:19-20, Paul writes, "That which is known about God is evident within them; for God made it evident to them. For since the creation of the world His invisible attributes, His eternal power and divine nature, have been clearly seen, being understood through what has been made, so that they are without excuse."

You and I have been given everything we need to experience what God longs for us to have more than anything else—an intimate relationship with Him.

God is infinite, so there is infinitely more of God than He has chosen to reveal. We are told in Deuteronomy 29:29 that "the secret things belong to the LORD our God, but the things revealed belong to us and to our sons forever, that we may observe all the words of this law." Francis Schaeffer emphasized the significance of the revelation of God in the titles of two of his books, *The God Who Is There* and *He Is There and He Is Not Silent.* God has spoken. Now the question is, will we hear and respond?

GENERAL REVELATION

The psalmist says, "The heavens are telling of the glory of God; and their expanse is declaring the work of His hands. Day to day pours forth speech, and night to night reveals knowledge" (Psalm 19:1-2). I have often told my Biola University theology classes that I like to think of general revelation seen in creation as God's multimedia. Just walk outside at sunset and gasp in amazement at the brilliant colors as the sun goes down. Look up to the skies late at night and see billions of stars, too many to count. What does that say about the God who created them? He is more powerful than the most powerful men on earth, for only He can create something out of nothing.

You can look at the intricate design of the human body with the skeletal formation, the blood vessels, the heart, the brain, and skin and discover that God is more wise and knowing and creative than the most brilliant men on earth. No human being can create a human body out of nothing.

Order does not come from chaos, and a design implies a Designer. Dr. Viggo Olsen embarked on a career of medicine and ultimately made a decision to give his life to Christ as a result of considering the order and design of God's creation. He imagined a theoretical experiment of throwing nine thousand wooden Scrabble pieces on the floor and realized they would never naturally fall in a discernible pattern, forming a story or a poem. The design must have a Designer. After surrendering his life to Christ, he declined a prestigious faculty position, moved to Bangladesh, and helped found the first modern medical facility there, Memorial Christian Hospital.

The order and design of God's creation provides visual evidence—a multimedia presentation—that helps you understand more clearly what you read in the Bible. C.S. Lewis wrote some very thought-provoking letters to Sheldon Vanauken, who included them in his book *A Severe Mercy.* In these letters, the brilliant Lewis pointed out profound lessons from God's creation. In one letter he told Vanauken that fish didn't complain about being in water because they were made for the water.[2] He used this argument to point out that humanity's desire or hunger for God is evidence that we were made to know God, that we are created for eternity. In the same letter, Lewis said that our discomfort with the passage of time is evidence that we are creatures made for eternity. We know from Ecclesiastes 3:11 that God has set eternity in our hearts. I love the way Lewis closes his letter, and I use his words often with those who are searching for God and engage in conversation with me: "But I think you are already in the meshes of the net! The Holy Spirit is after you. I doubt if you'll get away!"

If you have any doubts about God's designs on having you for Himself, simply look at the way Jesus pursued Paul. Paul was determined to persecute Christians and was traveling on the road to Damascus, intent on doing great damage to the church (Acts 9). Oh, how the Lord turned the tables on Paul. He met Paul on that Damascus road and spoke to him directly. Paul gave his life to Christ as a result of that experience and lived out the rest of his days for the Lord.

SPECIAL REVELATION

God revealed Himself not only generally in creation but also specifically in Christ. John tells us that "no one has seen God at any time; the only begotten God who is in the bosom of the Father, He has explained Him" (John 1:18). If you want to know what God is like, look at Jesus. Special revelation in Jesus means that He "has fully revealed the Father to a sinful humanity and through His redemption has enabled mankind to be restored to fellowship with God."[3] God's special revelation also extends to the Bible, for we know it is God-breathed (2 Timothy 3:16), written by men moved by the Holy Spirit (2 Peter 1:21), and living and active (Hebrews 4:12). The Bible may be thought of as God's love letter to us.

God's revelation of Himself was progressive and not given all at once, providing a new view of His nature at the first proclamation of each name. The Bible consists of an Old and a New Testament—66 books progressively given by God over a period of 1500 years, but "component parts of one divine revelation."[4] Thus, taking into account the whole counsel of God's Word is imperative and is reflected in the organization of this book. Augustine affirmed, "The New is in the Old concealed; the Old is in the New revealed."

A.B. Davidson points out in his *Theology of the Old Testament,* "But God could not make His moral nature known by mere statements concerning Himself delivered at once. His power He could reveal in one terrible act, but the principles lying behind His power, and governing the exercise of it—His justice, His goodness, His grace, in a word His moral nature—could not be shown except by a prolonged exhibition of Himself in relation to the life of men." It is one thing if God would have revealed Himself only once, but quite another to have shown the depth of His nature throughout history. The infinite, eternal God stepped into the limits of time to show Himself to you and to me.

THE REASON FOR REVELATION

God's revelation of Himself implies reason and purpose. There is one thing God desires—a relationship with you. Will you sit for a moment and contemplate the astounding and overwhelming greatness of this invitation? It comes from the God who created the universe, who created you, who holds all power in His hands, and who wants you to know Him, talk with Him, and live with Him. Not just now, but for all eternity. And He has given you every resource you need in order to know Him. He has made you for Himself. The way is clear for you to draw near to God that He may draw near to you (James 4:8).

You have discovered the fact that you are sinful and that your sins have separated you from a holy God. We know that "all have sinned and fall short of the glory of God" (Romans 3:23) and that the penalty of sin is death (Romans 6:23). The good news is that Jesus paid the penalty for your sin when He died on the cross (Romans 5:8). You are now free to enter into a relationship with God by receiving Jesus into your life. "But as many as received Him, to them He gave the right to become children of God, even to those who believe in His name" (John 1:12). If you have never received Christ and entered into a personal relationship with Him, you may pray a simple prayer like this one: *Lord Jesus, I need You. Thank You for dying on the cross for my sins. I ask You now to come into my life, forgive my sins, give me eternal life, and make me the person You want me to be. Amen.*

Entering into a relationship with God through Jesus is only the beginning of this great adventure of knowing God. You have the magnificent gift of the Bible, God's Word. Contained in the pages of God's love letter is His magnificent revelation of Himself to you. And how can you unlock the door to knowing God? By using the keys He has given you to know and love Him—His names. We will look more closely at the secret of the names of God tomorrow in day 3. As you engage in this 30-day journey, will you pray this prayer of Moses? "If you are pleased with me, teach me your ways so I may know you and continue to find favor with you" (Exodus 33:13 NIV). And may it be with you as it was with Moses—may the presence of the Lord go with you, and may He give you rest.

My Response

DATE:

KEY VERSE: "That which is known about God is evident within them; for God made it evident to them. For since the creation of the world His invisible attributes, His eternal power and divine nature, have been clearly seen, being understood through what has been made, so that they are without excuse" (Romans 1:19-20).

FOR FURTHER THOUGHT: What have you learned about God as you have observed His revelation in creation, in the Bible, and in Jesus? Write out one observation about God from creation, the Bible, and Jesus. Then close your time today by writing a prayer to the Lord, expressing all that is on your heart and thanking Him for revealing Himself to you.

MY RESPONSE:

Day Three

YOU CAN KNOW
HIS NAMES

The name of the LORD is a strong tower;
the righteous run to it and are safe.

PROVERBS 18:10 NIV

You can know God by His names. Names in the Bible are more than identification tags. A biblical name represents the person and explains the ways, character, and essence of that person. Old Testament names not only distinguished one person from another but also were "bound up closely with the person's very existence, representing and expressing his or her character and personality." Beyond that, learning a person's name meant entering into a relationship with him.[1]

Behind every name of God is His very presence and person. When God tells you His name, He is opening Himself to you in a new way so that you might know, love, and ultimately trust Him more completely. Each name of God is a great promise from Him for you to find, embrace, trust, and then live. In fact, the names of God are the greatest promises in the Bible. God is promising to you who He is and who He always will be, for He never changes. You can know that "the name of the LORD is a strong tower; the righteous run to it and are safe" (Proverbs 18:10 NIV). A whole world of faith and devotion is awaiting you in the names of God.

When you know the name of someone, you grow in your relationship with that person to a new and deeper level. Introducing oneself by name invites and implies relationship. Several years ago I was approached by a young woman at our church. She shyly walked up to me and introduced herself, "Hi, I'm Shelley." I took note of who she was, and a few weeks later, she attended one of our women's events.

I welcomed her and said, "Hi, Shelley, how are you today?"

She looked at me with surprise and said, "You remembered my name." I was actually surprised myself because I'm not that great at remembering names. Do you know what remembering Shelley's name meant to her? She realized anew God's love for her, and she began volunteering in our ministry. She is currently our women's ministries assistant, has begun new ministries of discipleship and Bible study, and is being used in a powerful way among the women at our church. What was one of the keys? Knowing and remembering her name.

God wants you to call Him by His name. Knowing God's names endears you to God. He loves to hear you call out to Him by His many names as He reveals them to you. This is real prayer to God as it is meant to be. In fact, throughout the Bible, you will discover that men and women often called on the name of the Lord (Genesis 4:26; 13:4; 16:13; 21:33).

Think about our use of names in earthly relationships. For example, my full name is Catherine Ellen Martin. My mother always calls me Catherine. When I was in trouble she would call out to me, "Catherine Ellen!" Those who are close to me, including my staff and other family members, call me Cath. I even have a blog, my online journal at www.cathsblog.com, that I call "Cath's Blog" because I want people to know me better. *Catherine* may sound formal to many, but it never seems formal to me when my mother calls me Catherine because of our intimate, close, precious relationship. If she called me Cathy, I wouldn't even answer because she doesn't know me as Cathy. I love to hear my mother call me Catherine. For me, her name is Mother. Not Mom or Ma, but Mother. The name *Mother* represents all that she is to me and our relationship from the time I was first born to now. And so it is with God—His names represent who He is to us and indicate the kind of relationship He desires with us.

Because God's names reveal His character, knowing those names unmasks His face, showing us who He is and what He looks like. We know that God spoke to Moses "face to face, as a man speaks with his friend" (Exodus 33:11 NIV). The phrase "face to face" in the context of God's relationship with Moses meant "heart to heart." God's face is who He is and His character, nature, ways, and personality.

We know that the Lord is one God—"Hear, O Israel: The LORD our God, the LORD is one" (Deuteronomy 6:4 NIV). Israel's neighbors had many gods, but Israel lived in the security and under the rule of their one God, the Creator of the universe, their King and Ruler. God is one, but He does have many facets, for He has many names. In fact, one poet has called Him the "God of a Thousand Names," signifying the unending facets of His character. God is infinite and therefore has unlimited attributes of character and personality. However, He has chosen to show us a relatively minute portion of Himself through His names discovered in Scripture. The numerous names of God reveal new facets of His character, and behind them all is the ineffable, immutable, holy, transcendent, majestic presence of God Himself, for God's name is equal to His presence.[2]

Knowing God's names reveals the many facets of your character as well. For example, knowing God as Elohim, your Creator, shows you the magnificent truth that you are created by God. I know Elizabeth Snyder as my mother. What does that say about me? I am her daughter. I also know my mother as my teacher. Because she is my teacher, I am her student. Because she truly loves me, I can know her as my intimate friend. Names reveal precious nuances of the nature of your relationship with God as you discover the facets of His character and your own.

God is issuing an invitation when He says, "Be still, and know that I am God" (Psalm 46:10). Do you know what He is asking of you? Stop everything, discover God, and then know Him. How can you do that? Through His names. Think of a treasure chest that is locked. Inside the treasure chest are unbelievable, countless riches. What you need is the key. To unlock the treasure chest of the character and personality of God you need the key that is wrapped up in knowing and trusting His names. God leans down to a level we can understand and reveals Himself to us through the multitude of His names. Not merely one name, but many; not one revelation, but a myriad. In doing so, He shows Himself to be a God who is not distant and hidden, but near and personal.

He does not show us Himself merely to give us information; He reveals Himself for the purpose of relationship. God wants an intimate relationship with you. And so He draws close to you and says, "I am..." so that you will draw close to Him and say, "You are..." And thus, there is interaction, experience, and a heart-to-heart relationship. As you grow in your knowledge of God's names, you will learn that He is more than you thought Him to be and beyond what you had imagined. He is good and kind and compassionate. He is also fierce and mighty and powerful. When you know Him as He really is, you will trust Him more than you trust anything or anyone else. He is completely reliable, unlike everything in the world that breaks down or lets you down.

The names of God enable and empower you. God asked Abraham to surrender his only son. How could he obey God and still save his son's life? Abraham knew that God was Yahweh-Jireh, "The Lord Will Provide." He said, "God will provide for Himself the lamb for the burnt offering" (Genesis 22:8).

Moses led the Israelite people in the Sinai desert for more than 40 years. How was he able to lead such a rebellious, and at times, idolatrous, ungodly people? Moses knew Yahweh, the I AM, the one who is and always will be, everything he needed for every circumstance of life (Exodus 3:14-15).

And David, a young boy who loved God, did what no other man in the Israelite army would even attempt. David killed the giant Goliath. How was he able to accomplish such a monumental task beyond his own abilities and strength? David knew El Shaddai, God Almighty, the one who is all-powerful and all-sufficient. David said to Goliath, "You come against me with sword and spear and javelin, but I come against you in the name of the LORD Almighty, the God of the armies of Israel, whom you have defied" (1 Samuel 17:45 NIV). God's names meet you wherever you are and in your deepest needs.

Dear friend, do you know the names of God? Do you know that God knows your name? God called Abram by name and eventually changed his name to Abraham. God called Moses by name from the burning bush. God called out to Samuel by his name. It is one thing for God to know your name but quite another for you to know God's names. Now is the time to draw near, discover the real person of God, and enter into a deeper, more intimate relationship with Him as He really is in light of His names. Leave your earthly cares at the door and step into the very courts of the King, the throne room of God, where, with your spiritual eyes of faith, you will see the Lord.

The Court of the King

With the staff that had failed in my need
Where the road had been stony and steep;
With lamp that was smoking and dim,
Though the darkness was growing more deep;
Weary, too weary to pray
And too heavy-hearted to sing,
Faint with the toils of the way
I came to the court of the King.
There where the fountains fall cool,
Their waters unfailing and pure;
There where the ministering palms
Stand like His promises sure,
Oh! There was peace in its shade,
Oh! There was rest in its calm;
And its sweet silences lay
On my bruised spirit like balm.
Long did I kneel in His court,
And walk in His garden so fair;
All I had lost or had lacked
I found in His treasuries there;
Oil to replenish my lamp,
His kindness a crown for my head,
For the staff that had wounded my hand
The rod of His mercy instead.
A garment of praises I found
For the sullen, dark garb I had worn,
And sandals of peace for the feet
That the rocks and the briers had torn;
Joy for my mourning He gave,
Making my spirit to sing,
And, girded with gladness and strength,
I passed from the court of the King.[3]

ANNIE JOHNSON FLINT

My Response

DATE:

KEY VERSE: "The name of the LORD is a strong tower; the righteous run to it and are safe" (Proverbs 18:10 NIV).

FOR FURTHER THOUGHT: What is the most significant truth you have learned about the names of God today? Why is it important to know the names of God? Write a prayer to the Lord, expressing your desire to know His names.

MY RESPONSE:

RESPONDING TO THE NAMES OF GOD

The people who know their God will display strength and take action.

DANIEL 11:32

Knowing God's names will change your life. When you learn a name of God, your new understanding of His character will inspire you to action. The revelation of God calls you to a deeper walk with Him and a greater demonstration of faith in Him. Seeing God in a new way can be overwhelming as you realize He is so much more than you thought He was or knew Him to be. Your new vision of God is humbling. When you learn something new about God, you may feel that with so much to know of Him, you don't really know Him at all. And so, dear friend, be humbled. And be bold. God has shown you Himself because He intends for you to act on what you now know to be true. Daniel discovered that "the people who know their God will display strength and take action" (Daniel 11:32).

When I was in high school, I received good grades except in one class—algebra. I simply could not understand algebra. My mother suggested I stay after school and be tutored by my teacher. I wasn't thrilled with the idea, but I knew I had no other choice because of my difficulty understanding what to me was a mysterious mathematical process. My teacher, Mrs. Tryon, spent many hours showing me the principles of calculating with mathematical equations. Algebra uses variables that never change. During my tutoring sessions, I learned how to calculate in the context of equations using those unchanging variables. Said another way, to calculate, I learned to figure those unchanging variables into the appropriate equations.

You and I must learn to calculate the names of God into our very lives. Oswald Chambers says, "All our fret and worry is caused by calculating without God," and "The one thing that keeps us from the possibility of worrying is bringing God in as the greatest factor in all our calculations… Haul yourself up a hundred and one times a day in order to do it, until you get into the habit of putting God first and calculating with Him in view."[1] Paul calls this calculation walking "by faith, not by sight" (2 Corinthians 5:7). Walking by faith in God's names means you consider God, His very person and His presence, in the heat of your emotion and in the fire of your trial.

Hebrews 11, faith's hall of fame, lists one person after another who, when faced with impossible obstacles, considered God—they calculated Him as the greatest factor in the midst of their difficulties and triumphed in faith. Noah considered God's warning about an impending flood as more true than the ever-present world around him, and as a result, he obeyed God and built an ark (Hebrews 11:7). God's words proved to be true; He did bring about a flood that destroyed everyone except Noah and his family. Abraham trusted God's promise to lead and guide him, leaving the comforts of home for an unknown country (Hebrews 11:8). He considered God as the great factor in his life to the point of living in a tent and trusting God to carry out His promise. God indeed did fulfill His promise and made Abraham a great nation and took his descendants into the promised land, a land flowing with milk and honey.

And now, friend, what about you? What is your circumstance today? Have you learned the art of calculating the names of God as the greatest factor in your life? Do you hear the call of God to launch out in faith, trusting who God says He is in the midst of your own situation? When you respond by faith in God's names, you will live a more purposeful, satisfying, and victorious life than those who do not know His names. You will see that you have an alternative to the typical worry, despair, and discouragement that many of our circumstances tempt us to entertain.

Calculating God as the great factor in life, this walking by faith, results in a variety of responses by the people of God. When you study the Bible, you will discover that the people of God called upon the name of God (Genesis 26:25), praised the name of God (Psalm 69:30), confessed the name of God (1 Kings 8:33), blessed the name of God (Daniel 2:20), walked in the name of God (Micah 4:5), and ultimately, trusted in the name of God (Psalm 9:10). David says in Psalm 20:7 (NIV), "Some trust in chariots and some in horses, but we trust in the name of the LORD our God." David calculated the name of God as the greatest factor in his life, not chariots and horses or any other thing.

You need to know that God is heartbroken when His people do not seek Him, respond to Him, call on Him, or trust Him. Listen to these words of God in Isaiah 65:1-2:

> I permitted Myself to be sought by those who did not ask for Me; I permitted Myself to be found by those who did not seek Me. I said, "Here am I, here am I," to a nation which did not call on My name. I have spread out My hands all day long to a rebellious people, who walk in the way which is not good, following their own thoughts.

Can you hear and understand the heart of God when you read these words? Do you hear the depth of feeling and emotion in God when His people do not call on His name?

When God gives us His names, He is calling out to us, asking for a response from us. When we do respond, we are changed forever. You will become like David, who said, "You, LORD, keep my lamp burning; my God turns my darkness into light. With your help I can advance against a troop; with my God I can scale a wall" (Psalm 18:28-29 TNIV). Faith and trust are like muscles that grow with use. Hanging on to God in the midst of your storms in life is like anchoring yourself to a rock that cannot be moved. Even though the waters rage about you, you endure, and you make it through to the other side of your trial.

When I lived in Dallas, I was in a head-on automobile accident, and an ambulance rushed me to the local hospital. Lying on the hospital table, I was told that the large laceration of my scalp would need sutures, and that meant giving me local anesthesia. When I felt the stinging of the needle, my mind leaped to Jesus experiencing the crown of thorns prior to His crucifixion. Then I thought of El Roi, the God who sees me and who promised to never leave me, saying, "Do not fear, for I am with you; do not anxiously look about you, for I am your God. I will strengthen you, surely I will help you, surely I will uphold you with My righteous right hand" (Isaiah 41:10). I began thanking the Lord that He was right there with me and promised to give me strength. My heart calmed with the assurance of His presence. My experience with God there in that emergency room in Dallas so many years ago has served to encourage me many times over the years when faced with impossible situations. When you trust God in the storms of life, your history with God becomes a platform on which you can stand in future difficulties. These experiences help you remember your God and what He can and will do for you.

Robert Louis Stevenson tells of a storm that caught a vessel off a rocky coast and threatened to drive it and its passengers to destruction. In the midst of the terror, one daring man, contrary to orders, went to the deck and made the dangerous passage to the pilothouse. He saw the captain at his post holding the wheel unwaveringly, and inch by inch, turning the ship out, once more, to sea. The pilot smiled at the man. Then, the daring passenger went below and shouted out a note of cheer: "I have seen the face of the pilot, and he smiled. All is well." When you respond to the names of God in trust, it is as though you have seen the face of your heavenly Pilot, and you will be able to smile and say, "All is well."

DATE:

KEY VERSE: "The people who know their God will display strength and take action" (Daniel 11:32).

FOR FURTHER THOUGHT: In what ways have you responded to God over the last year? How important is it to respond to God's names? What is the most important truth you have learned today?

MY RESPONSE:

HOW TO TRUST IN THE NAMES OF GOD

Those who know Your name
will put their trust in You.
PSALM 9:10

Knowing God's names is the secret to trusting God. David, the man after God's own heart, knew this powerful secret and was a champion at trusting God. He spoke often about trust, perhaps more than anyone else in the Bible. The word translated "trust" in the New American Standard Bible is mentioned 129 times, more than 40 times in Psalms alone, mostly by David. David expressed his knowledge of the secret of trusting God's names when he said, "Those who know Your name will put their trust in You" (Psalm 9:10). The Hebrew word translated "trust" is *batach* and refers to reliance or belief in a person or object. David is saying that when you know God's name, you will rely on Him and believe in Him.

Mrs. Charles Cowman tells the story of the catacombs, the underground tombs of the early church, where modern-day explorers take a thread with them through all the dark passages and tortuous windings, and by this thread find their way back again to the light. God's names form the thread you can rely on in the dark corridors of life. They will steer you to the light of God's love and the power of His strength. In this regard, I like to think of TRUST as Total Reliance Under Stress and Trial.

David writes about trust often in Psalms. Because I try to read a psalm every day, I am often in Psalms, so I have taken note of his frequent mention of trust. One day, while studying the names of God, I happened to read Psalm 103, one of the psalms of David. I read verse 8: "The LORD is compassionate and gracious, slow to anger and abounding in lovingkindness." My eyes were immediately drawn back to the page, where I did a double take on verse 8. *I've read that phrase somewhere,* I thought to myself. Then I remembered the words the Lord declared when He passed by Moses, declaring His name: "The LORD, the LORD God, compassionate and gracious, slow to anger, and abounding in lovingkindness and truth; who keeps lovingkindness for thousands, who forgives iniquity, transgression and sin" (Exodus 34:6).

The match in the words was too exact to be a coincidence. I realized a very powerful truth—David knew the names of God. And he not only knew the names of God but also declared them often. I began to detect in David's psalms a pattern for trusting in God through His names. First, at some point in David's journey, he *discovered* the names of God, one by one, on his pilgrimage with the Lord as God taught him about Himself. He could not have known God's names as he described in Psalm 9:10 had he not learned them from God.

Second, David *drew near* to God's names, learning God's ways and character through time alone with Him. His prayer was, "Make me know Your ways, O LORD; teach me Your paths. Lead me in Your truth and teach me, for You are the God of my salvation; for You I wait all the day" (Psalm 25:4-5).

Third, David *declared* the names of God: "I will tell of Your name to my brethren" (Psalm 22:22). He declared God's names not only to others but also to God in his prayers. We see a perfect example of this declaration in Psalm 103:8, our theme verse for today. He also declared God's names to himself: "The LORD is my light and my salvation; whom shall I fear?" (Psalm 27:1).

Fourth, David also *depended* on God's names. "Some trust in chariots and some in horses, but we trust in the name of the LORD our God" (Psalm 20:7 NIV).

Finally, David *delighted* in the names of God: "O LORD, our Lord, how majestic is Your name in all the earth, who have displayed your splendor above the heavens!" (Psalm 8:1). "Therefore I will give thanks to You among the nations, O LORD, and I will sing praises to Your name" (Psalm 18:49). "I will praise the name of God with song and magnify Him with thanksgiving" (Psalm 69:30).

When I saw that David discovered, drew near to, declared, depended on, and delighted in the names of God, I thought to myself, *No wonder David was such a champion at trusting God!* No wonder he was able to say, "O my God, in You I trust" (Psalm 25:2). "I have trusted in the LORD without wavering" (Psalm 26:1). "The LORD is my strength and my shield; my heart trusts in Him, and I am helped" (Psalm 28:7). "As for me, I trust in You, O LORD, I say, 'You are my God'" (Psalm 31:14). Suddenly I realized God was showing me how to trust in Him through His names. The pattern of discovering His names, drawing near to His names, declaring His names, depending on His names, and finally, delighting in His names was the key to unlock the door of ever-increasing trust in God. I even designed a page for the *Quiet Time Notebook* to help me apply what I was learning to my life (see appendix 2).

What difference will it make to trust in the names of God? You will move from being an observer to becoming a participant, experiencing God for yourself and walking with Him in your daily life. Hannah Whitall Smith, in her book *The God of All Comfort,* tells the story of a man who was involved in ministry and, as a result, had developed a great reputation for piety. Unfortunately, he also had a bad temper and a sharp tongue. Finally, for some unknown reason, a change seemed to come over him, and he was sweet, gentle, and kind to everyone. At last one of his friends approached him and asked if he had changed his religion. He said, "No, I have not changed my religion. I have, at last, let my religion change me."[1]

When you trust the names of God by discovering His names, drawing near to His names, declaring His names, depending on His names, and delighting in His names, you will see God work in your life in amazing ways. You will be like Hezekiah, who "trusted in the LORD, the God of Israel; so that after him there was none like him among all the kings of

Judah, nor among those who were before him. For he clung to the LORD; he did not depart from following Him, but kept His commandments" (2 Kings 18:5-6). Oh, there is an immense value in trusting the Lord.

Trusting in the Lord is your greatest response in a time of trial, trouble, loss, or need. Whatever your stress, whatever your trial, rely on God in the midst of your need, and watch to see what God will accomplish. Sometimes He will surprise you with answers you could never have asked or imagined.

John Bunyan spent 12 long years in a jail in Bedford, England. There he completed his best and greatest literary work, *Pilgrim's Progress,* one of the bestsellers of all time. Bunyan's comment betrays his trust in God when he says, "I was at home in prison and sat me down and wrote, and wrote, for joy did make me write." Even in a prison cell, you can trust in the Lord, and the result can lead you, like Paul and Silas, to sing (Acts 16:25).

Perhaps, even now, you are in a prison of sorts, where you need to rely on the one who is greater than yourself because you have discovered that you are not enough for what you are facing. But you may be approaching your finest hour, where you will discover God's names, draw near to His names, declare His names, depend on His names, and delight in His names. Others may say it is over for you, but God never says such words. He is waiting for you to draw near and know Him as you have never known Him before and then to trust Him as you have never trusted before. Such an act of trust is never easy, but it is possible. Calculate God into your circumstances as the greatest factor of all and then watch to see what He will accomplish.

Recently a dear friend faced the possibility of a recurrence of lymphoma. She went to the hospital for a biopsy, and then we waited for the results for more than a week. I had many conversations with God about my friend's test results. I told God what I wanted. I asked God for healing. I explained to God what I felt was important. And finally, I cast my great care for my friend into the arms of the Lord and said, "Lord, El Shaddai, my sufficiency, I trust You completely with my friend." I just received a phone call that the biopsy results show that the growth is benign. I saw God work in my heart, teaching me anew to trust Him with the outcome of events. He is the one in control, and He is perfectly confident in carrying out His plan. I learned that no difficulty is overcome by me alone but by God.

Thomas Gainsborough, the English artist of portraits and landscapes, longed to be a musician. He bought many musical instruments and tried to play them. He even bought a violin that a great violinist had owned and played. He thought that if he had that instrument, he would also be able to play the violin. But he learned that the music was not in the violin but in the master who played it. And so it is with God—He can produce beautiful music in your life regardless of what you face today. What is the secret? Trusting in the names of God.

My Response

DATE:

KEY VERSE: "Those who know Your name will put their trust in You" (Psalm 9:10).

FOR FURTHER THOUGHT: What is the most significant truth you have learned today about trusting God? How does knowing God's names help you trust Him?

MY RESPONSE:

Day Six

QUIET TIME WEEK ONE: KNOWING GOD'S NAMES

LORD, there is no one like you to help the powerless against the mighty. Help us, O LORD our God, for we rely on you, and in your name we have come against this vast army. LORD, you are our God; do not let mere mortals prevail against you.

2 CHRONICLES 14:11 TNIV

PREPARE YOUR HEART

This week you have been learning all about the names of God and what it means to know them and therefore to know Him. The Bible is full of great examples of men and women who knew God. The result of their knowing God's name was always a great trust in Him, especially when faced with difficulties in life. When you are in the heat of the battle, what can you do and what will God do? Today you will have the opportunity to look at real-life examples of those who trusted the names of God. Turn to God now and ask Him to quiet your heart and speak to you in His Word.

READ AND STUDY GOD'S WORD

1. Today you are going to look briefly at two men who knew God's names and trusted Him. Look at the following verses and record what you learn about King Hezekiah and King Asa.

2 Kings 18:5—King Hezekiah

2 Chronicles 14:1-15—King Asa

2. Notice in 2 Chronicles 14:11 (NIV) that Asa prayed to the Lord, "LORD, there is no one like you to help the powerless against the mighty. Help us, O LORD our God, for we rely on you, and in your name we have come against this vast army." The Hebrew for "rely on" is another word for trust and means to lean on and support oneself. Notice the close relationship here in the heat of the battle between reliance on God and His name. There is strength for you, dear friend, in the name of the Lord. Look at the following verses and write out what you learn about God's names.

Psalm 8:1

Psalm 31:3

Psalm 48:10

Psalm 54:1

Psalm 75:1

Psalm 80:18

Psalm 135:13

3. Summarize in two or three sentences what you have learned about God's names.

ADORE GOD IN PRAYER

Talk with the Lord today about your desire to know Him and His names. Tell Him why you want to know Him more.

YIELD YOURSELF TO GOD

Meditate on these words from *Quotes from the Quiet Hour:*

> I had walked life's way with an easy tread;
> I had followed where comfort and pleasure led,
> Until one day in a quiet place,
> I met my Master face to face.

> With station and wealth and rank for a goal,
> Much thought for the body, but none for the soul,
> I had sworn to win in life's made race—
> Till I met my Master face to face.

> I had built my castles and reared them high,
> Till their domes had touched the blue of the sky;
> I had sworn to rule with an iron mace,
> Till I met my Master face to face.

> I met Him and knew Him, and blushed to see
> His eyes full of love were fixed upon me;
> And I faltered and fell at His feet that day,
> And my castles melted and vanished away;

Melted and vanished, and in their place,
I saw naught else but my Master's face.

My thought is now for the souls of men;
I have lost my life to find it again,
Ever since that day in a quiet place,
I met my Master face to face.[1]

ENJOY HIS PRESENCE

Think about the difference knowing the Lord has made in your own life. What situation are you facing today that requires the kind of trust King Hezekiah demonstrated and the kind of prayer that King Asa prayed in the heat of the battle? Write a prayer to the Lord, expressing all that is on your heart, and put your reliance on the Lord your God.

REST IN HIS LOVE

"Hezekiah trusted in the LORD, the God of Israel. There was no one like him among all the kings of Judah, either before him or after him. He held fast to the LORD and did not cease to follow him; he kept the commands the LORD had given Moses. And the LORD was with him; he was successful in whatever he undertook" (2 Kings 18:5-7 NIV).

Notes—Week One

Week Two

TRUSTING IN GOD'S NAMES

Days 7–12

Day Seven

DISCOVER HIS NAMES

Jacob said, "Please tell me your name."
GENESIS 32:29 NIV

There is no greater discovery in life than the discovery of God. In the heart of every person is a desire for God, a hunger that only God Himself can satisfy. Blaise Pascal, seventeenth-century mathematician, philosopher, and believer in Jesus Christ, alluded to the oft-mentioned "God-shaped vacuum" in section 7 of his *Pensées*. "The infinite abyss can only be filled by an infinite and immutable Object; that is to say, only by God Himself." Augustine, in his *Confessions,* declared, "You have made us for Yourself, and our hearts are restless, until they rest in You."

Paul, in his sermon on Mars Hill, addressed those living in Athens as "very religious in all respects." Citing their altar "TO AN UNKNOWN GOD," he proclaimed, "So you are ignorant of the very thing you worship—and this is what I am going to proclaim to you" (Acts 17:23 TNIV). That certainly got the attention of the Athenians, famed for their learning, philosophy, and fine arts. God as Creator, God as provider, God as infinite, God as self-sufficient, and God as author of nations—in a few short sentences, this sermon to the heathens demanded repentance from idolatry and allegiance to an UNKNOWN GOD, who is "Lord of heaven and earth." Finally, Paul appealed to and admonished his audience. He proclaimed, "God did this so that men would seek him and perhaps reach out for him and find him, though he is not far from each one of us. For in him we live and move and have our being" (Acts 17:22-28 NIV). Paul left no doubt that we are created to seek God, know God, and live with God. And so our prayer must be Jacob's prayer the night he wrestled with God: "Please, tell me your name" (Genesis 32:29 NIV).

When we ask God to tell us His name, we ask to know Him as He really is. Believing in anything other than God as He is will take you on a detour to idolatry. God's first great commandment is this: "You shall have no other gods before Me. You shall not make for yourself an idol, or any likeness of what is in heaven above or on earth beneath or in the water under the earth. You shall not worship them or serve them; for I, the LORD your God, am a jealous God" (Exodus 20:3-5).

God makes His feelings clear about idolatry through Isaiah's words to the people of Israel when they worshipped other gods: "Their land has also been filled with idols; They worship the work of their hands, that which their fingers have made" (Isaiah 2:8). Any idol, whether people or possessions, money or entertainment, position or prestige, cannot save you from your sins, give you eternal life, or satisfy the deepest needs of your heart. You are made for God alone. Therefore, our discovery of God is based on His revelation of Himself. And the authority for our belief is grounded solely in God and His Word.

I was flipping through the television channels one day when an infomercial caught my eye. A barefoot man stood on a stage in front of a large audience, claiming his words would change their lives. Since I was in the midst of writing about the Lord, who does indeed change lives, I paused to hear what this man had to say. I listened for at least 15 minutes while he quoted poets and philosophers who believed people could change their own lives. As I listened, I was struck with the stark contrast of this man's philosophy and the words of the one true God of the Bible.

Our culture constantly tempts us to believe in many conflicting and irrational things that result in idolatry. How often have we heard television commentators mention the "golf gods" or the "weather gods"? Many times I have heard talk-show hosts spout their own opinion: "Well, God would never do that!" The barefoot guru on television would probably counter, "What I believe works for me." And I would answer, "Does it really? For how long?" You see, anything that is not true is a lie. If you have faith in a lie, eventually that lie will fail you. I would respond to the guru by saying that even though something seems to be working at the moment, it may not ultimately be trustworthy. Anything apart from God that "works" for someone only works for a while and eventually fails. God Himself and what He says motivates and determines our beliefs.[1]

One day, while reading Psalm 84, I decided to slow down and write out everything I observed about God. When I read verse 8, I wrote out "God of Jacob." And then I stopped and thought about that name. What did Jacob learn about God? I turned to Genesis and read the entire account of his life. I discovered that Jacob was not only resourceful but also a manipulator, constantly trying to bend circumstances to benefit his life. He finally arrived at a point where he was completely without resources. Only then did he discover that God was his power and strength—stronger than he could ever hope to become. Discovering the name *God of Jacob* was meaningful to me and taught me to rely on God's resources rather than my own. God custom designed this powerful discovery of one of His names through Jacob. I learned that I, like Jacob, can sometimes be too resourceful for my own good. I have often reflected on the *God of Jacob* name when I have been without resources in my own life and have remembered God's unlimited resources.

How can you discover God's names? As you read your Bible each day, always look for truths about God. Following a Bible reading plan is the best way to discover who God is, what He does, and what He says. You may use a devotional Bible, a book of the Bible, or even an organized Bible study. I like to divide a journal page in my *Quiet Time Notebook* into three sections—who God is, what God does, and what God says—and then write out my observations from a passage of Scripture. (See appendix 2 for an example of an observation study on the names of God in a passage of Scripture.)

Here are some examples of the truths you can record about God as you read His Word each day:

• His names—"the God who sees me" (Genesis 13:16 NIV).

- His character—"His compassions never fail" (Lamentations 3:22).

- His attributes—"You shall be holy, for I am holy" (1 Peter 1:16).

- His ways and works—"The Lord gives grace and glory" (Psalm 84:11).

- His words—"Do not fear, for I am with you" (Isaiah 41:10).

In addition to your daily Bible reading plan, you can use tools like these to discover God's names:

- A topical concordance, such as *Nave's Topical Bible.* Under the topic *God* you will discover a list of verses that describe God's character qualities and attributes. Those verses will also reveal names of God.

- A Bible dictionary, such as the *New Bible Dictionary* or *Unger's Bible Dictionary.* You will find information on the names of God under the topics *Name* and *God.*

- A Bible encyclopedia, such as *The Zondervan Pictorial Encyclopedia of the Bible* or the *International Standard Bible Encyclopedia.* Look up *God* and *Name* to find names of God.

- Theological books that discuss the names, attributes, and character of God are included in the recommended reading list in appendix 2.

- Bible studies, such as this book's eight-week companion book of quiet times, *Trusting in the Names of God—A Quiet Time Experience.*

Once you have discovered a name or attribute of God, write what you have learned. In the course of my studies, I have designed special "Trusting in the Names of God" devotional Bible study pages for the *Quiet Time Notebook* (available from Quiet Time Ministries), but your journal or lined notebook paper will work as well. When you first discover a name of God, write out the name and the Hebrew or Greek transliteration, citing a significant verse and its historical context. Using a word-study tool such as the

Hebrew-Greek Key Word Study Bible by Zodhiates or the *NASB Exhaustive Concordance,* write a definition and description.

For example, in Genesis 1:1 we discover the first mention of God: "In the beginning God…" In the *Hebrew-Greek Key Word Study Bible,* at Genesis 1:1, above the word *God* is the number 430. That number is from A.H. Strong's numbering system of all the words in the Bible. Simply look up 430 in the Hebrew dictionary in the back of the *Hebrew-Greek Key Word Study Bible,* and you will discover the Hebrew name for God, *Elohim,* with a definition. If you use an exhaustive Bible concordance, simply look up the word *God,* identify the number (430) to the right of Genesis 1:1, and look in the Hebrew dictionary for 430.[2] After you have determined the definition for the name, read the surrounding verses and summarize the historical situation. (See appendix 2 and figure 1 for examples.)

Discovering God's names and attributes alters the course of your life. At the age of 15, Duncan Campbell, walking home after a dance, passed by the church where he attended Sunday school. The lights were on, and a prayer meeting was in progress. Campbell went into the meeting and saw that his father was there. He sat down next to his father, who was praying at the time. One of the evangelists read Job 33:14 (KJV), "For God speaketh once, yea twice, yet man perceiveth it not." This realization of the existence of God, the presence of God, and the person of God was so astonishing and convicting that Duncan got up and ran out of the service. Stopping twice on the way home, he fell to his knees and asked for mercy.

He arrived home in the early hours of the morning and found his mother on her knees praying for him. Still unsettled, he secluded himself in the barn and prayed, thinking about the words of John 5:24 (KJV): "He that heareth my word, and believeth on him that sent me, hath everlasting life, and shall not come into condemnation; but is passed from death unto life." Realizing those words were the very Word of God, the God who speaks, he immediately surrendered his life to Christ. With great joy, Duncan ran to the kitchen and told his mother the wonderful news. They knelt together to pray, and his mother cried out, "Oh God, You are still the God who answers prayer!"[3] Duncan Campbell grew up to become a great evangelist and was instrumental in the Lewis Revival of 1949 in Scotland.

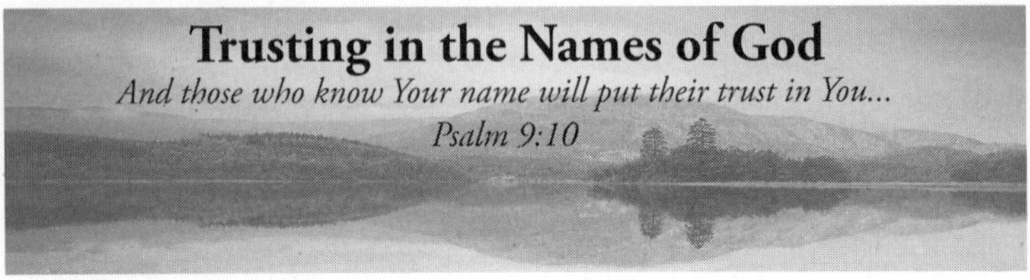

Discover His Name

Name or attribute of God: God

Hebrew or Greek transliteration: Elohim, elohiym

Significant verse(s): Genesis 1:1

Historical context: Creation

Strong's number(s): 430

Definition and description of name or attribute of God: the true God, masculine plural form, occurs 2600 times in the OT, conveys in Scripture that God is Creator, King, Judge, Lord, and Savior. He is faithful, gracious, and compassionate.

FIGURE 1

DATE:

KEY VERSE: "Jacob said, 'Please tell me your name'" (Genesis 32:29 NIV).

FOR FURTHER THOUGHT: Why is it important to know God as He is? What is your daily Bible reading plan (do you use a devotional Bible, a book of the Bible, or a Bible study)? What method of discovering God's names are you going to try?

MY RESPONSE:

DRAW NEAR
TO HIS NAMES

Draw near to God and He
will draw near to you.

JAMES 4:8

aking time to draw near to God gives you a new view of His character. James promises that when you draw near to God, He will draw near to you (James 4:8). The Greek word translated "draw near" is *engizo* and means to approach and come near—in this case, to come near to God. Another rendering states it this way, "Come to meet God, and he will come and stay close to you."¹ What an incredible promise we have in this verse—if we approach and come near to God, He will come near to us.

I have the most amazing gadget for my car—an FM transmitter that allows my iPod audio to play through my car speakers. This little transmitter allows me to listen to sermons while I drive. But when I first installed the transmitter I couldn't get it to work. The iPod was playing, but I couldn't hear anything. I could even see the sermon information on the screen of the player, but still no sound. Finally I realized I needed to tune in the radio to the same FM frequency as the transmitter attached to my player.

And so it is with our relationship with God. We must slow down to tune in to Him. Drawing near to God means to turn the dial away from frequencies that crowd the bandwidth of our heart and mind and tune in to what God is saying in His Word. Tune out the job challenges, financial worries, and relationship difficulties and tune in to the depth and beauty of the name or attribute of God. Drawing near means setting aside a time with God, a quiet place with God, and then a plan for your quiet time alone with Him.

How can you draw near to God's names?

Use a concordance to look at other occurrences of the name of God or attribute you want to study. For example, in my study of *the God of Jacob*, I found many helpful verses simply by looking up the word *Jacob* in my concordance and then finding the phrase *God of Jacob*. Taking time with these verses showed me that the God of Jacob appeared to Moses (Exodus 4:5), anointed King David (2 Samuel 23:1), sets me securely on high in the day of trouble (Psalm 20:1), is my stronghold (Psalm 46:7), is worthy of praise (Psalm 75:9), and hears my prayer (Psalm 84:8).

Use *The Treasury of Scripture Knowledge* to cross-reference the verse where you have discovered the name of God. Cross-references will help you identify the background of the name or attribute of God and find other occurrences.

Consult commentaries by Matthew Henry, Frank Gaebelein, and others to discover what scholars have written about the verse or passage of Scripture containing the name or attribute of God.

Read about the name of God or attribute you are studying in the *New Bible Dictionary, International Standard Bible Encyclopedia,* and other Bible dictionaries and encyclopedias.

Consult other books discussing the name of God or attribute you are studying such as *Knowing God* by J.I. Packer, *Names of God* by Nathan Stone, and others.

Write your discoveries in your journal or in the "Trusting in the Names of God" devotional Bible pages for the *Quiet Time Notebook* (see appendix 2 and figure 2 for examples). Your discoveries might include a list of significant verses or a short phrase summarizing an interesting idea or unique perspective. Howard Vos, an Old Testament scholar, asserts, "When it comes to Scripture, one must stop just casually looking and must start to *see.* True sight or perception will sometimes involve the use of a pencil and even some tabulation."[2] Writing out your insights from the Word of God will help you to think deeply about God and respond to the Holy Spirit's work in your life.

Slow down and take time to think about what you are learning. Frederick Faber writes,

> Within a thought so great, our souls
> Little and modest grow,
> And, by its vastness awed, we learn
> The art of walking slow.

We need to learn this art of walking slow, slow enough to think great thoughts. Great thoughts rarely materialize out of thin air. Time is required if we would, as Tozer urges us, drink deeply at the fountain of living water, delight in His presence, and experience "the inner sweetness of the very God Himself in the core and center" of our hearts.[3] Tozer states, "Without doubt, the mightiest thought the mind can entertain is the thought of God, and the weightiest word in any language is its word for God."[4]

Alan Redpath related that in the spring months in Chicago, if you had ventured down to the shores of Lake Michigan early in the morning, you would have seen a man facedown on the beach, often worshipping God for more than an hour. That praying man was none other than the busy pastor of Southside Alliance Church, editor of the *Alliance Weekly* magazine, and author of *The Pursuit of God,* A.W. Tozer. Tozer lived what he wrote; he wanted to know God more than he wanted any other thing in his life.

Henri Nouwen, author, teacher, and priest, points to the heart of the spiritual dangers we face in our culture:

> Our society is not a community radiant with the love of Christ, but a dangerous network of domination and manipulation in which we can easily get entangled and lose our soul. The basic question is whether we ministers of Jesus Christ have not already been so deeply molded by the seductive powers of our dark world that we have become blind to our own and other people's fatal state and have lost the power and motivation to swim for our lives.[5]

Nouwen concludes, "Solitude is the furnace of transformation," encouraging each one of us to create space in our lives where God can act. We need to be still and know that He is God (Psalm 46:10 NIV). Josef Pieper, in speaking of the need for leisure, declares, "It is in these silent receptive moments that the soul of man is sometimes visited by an awareness of what holds the world together."[6] And of course, here we are speaking of an awareness of God Himself. Don Postema, in his book *Space for God*, motivates us to cultivate this attitude of quiet:

> Such an attitude pits us against compulsive busyness, against drivenness. It leads toward solitude and contemplation—toward creating an inner receptivity, a space where we can hear our deepest longings, realize what life is about, penetrate into reality. It can mean making space for God.[7]

Biblical solitude and contemplation is never accomplished in a vacuum and always focuses on God as He has revealed Himself in His creation, in Jesus, and in the Word of God.

My friend Jim Smoke, busy pastor and author, is a master at creating space for God in his life. His office is located next to mine at our church, and we often share our discoveries of God. I'll walk to his door and softly knock. I'll hear him turn in his chair, grab the doorknob, and open the door. He looks at me with his big smile and says, "Come in, Catherine. Have a seat!" I see one or two books lying open on his desk, along with an open Bible. His example of slowing down for God speaks volumes to me and so many others who have the privilege of knowing him.

Even Jesus demonstrated this art of "walking slow" and getting away from the noise to draw near to His Father in a quiet place. His withdrawing to draw near is seen most clearly in Luke 5:15-16: "But the news about Him continued to spread, and great crowds were gathering to hear Him and to be cured of their diseases. But Jesus Himself continued His habit of retiring to lonely spots and praying."[8] If quiet time and solitude to draw near to the Father is important to Jesus, it should be all the more important to us if we would launch out on this great adventure of knowing God.

One day in my quiet time I was drawing near to God to learn more about the name *God of Jacob*. I saw truths I had never seen before. What stood out to me in particular was the wrestling match between the Lord and Jacob. That incident in the Bible has always puzzled me. I had never before taken time to think about it. Now I thought about how Jacob was truly alone, away from everyone he knew and loved. He was terrified about the prospect of meeting his brother, whom he had betrayed so many years before. Life experiences had come and gone for Jacob. He was not the young man who had run for his life so long ago, in danger from his angry brother, Esau. Jacob, now married with children and owner of many possessions, was on his way back home. He had been the resourceful one, but now he was feeling utterly helpless. And so the Lord met him on a lonely island that night. God didn't have a long talk with Jacob. He didn't take him on a trip to a new place. No, He wrestled with Jacob.

As I thought long and hard about this event, I asked myself, *What is the significance of God's choice to wrestle? What happens when you wrestle with someone?* Then it came to me. One thing always stands out in a wrestling match between two opponents—the strength, intelligence, and experience of one versus the other. In this case, because Jacob wrestled with the Lord, Jacob discovered something about God that until that night he had denied because he constantly relied on himself. That night Jacob discovered God was more powerful. Jacob left the wrestling match with a greater knowledge of God—and a dislocated hip as a reminder.

Jacob is included in the hall of fame of faith in Hebrews 11, and we are told, "By faith Jacob, as he was dying, blessed each of the sons of Joseph, and worshiped, leaning on the top of his staff" (Hebrews 11:21). What a reminder to Jacob of the strength and power of God, strong enough to lean on regardless of the challenge he faced in life. What a discovery of God for me in the name *God of Jacob.* The Lord showed me He is strong enough to trust regardless of the circumstances. Such are the discoveries awaiting us when we walk slow and draw near to the names of God.

Trusting in the Names of God

Those who know Your name will put their trust in You.

Psalm 9:10

Discover His Name

Name or attribute of God: *God*

Hebrew or Greek transliteration: *Elohim, elohiym*

Significant verse(s): *Genesis 1:1*

Historical context: *Creation*

Strong's number(s): *430*

Definition and description of name or attribute of God: *the true God, masculine plural form, occurs 2600 times in the OT, conveys in Scripture that God is Creator, King, Judge, Lord, and Savior. He is faithful, gracious, and compassionate.*

Draw Near to His Name

Digging deeper—significant verses, reference tools, including commentaries, dictionaries, encyclopedias, books on names and character of God:

Genesis 5:1; Deuteronomy 4:31; 7:9; Psalm 47:7-8; 50:6; 86:12; 116:5; Hosea 13:4

UBS Handbook: Only word for "God" found in the story of creation.

Lockyer: Plurality in unity, occurs 35 times in the first 2 chapters of Genesis, mostly in connection with God's creative power. Used most often in Deuteronomy and Psalms.

Nathan Stone: Expresses general idea of greatness and glory.

William MacDonald: Elohim is self-existent and uncreated.

FIGURE 2

DATE:

KEY VERSE: "Draw near to God and He will draw near to you" (James 4:8).

FOR FURTHER THOUGHT: What was the most important thought you had today as you read? What will you need to do in your own life to slow down and draw near to God?

MY RESPONSE:

Day Nine

DECLARE
HIS NAMES

I will declare your name to my people;
in the assembly I will praise you.

PSALM 22:22 TNIV

Saying what you believe about God's name affirms its truth in your heart. An affirmation is the assertion that something exists or is true. Affirmations in the Bible occur as solemn declarations that serve the same purpose as a commitment, implying a pledge, promise, or obligation. When I read the psalms of David, that great champion of trusting God, I am impressed by the repeated affirmations of what he believes. If you want to read King David's statement of faith, read the psalms of David.

Many of David's affirmations of belief are presented as prayers to God as he declared God's name. "Answer me when I call to you, my righteous God" (Psalm 4:1 TNIV). "Lᴏʀᴅ, our Lord, how majestic is your name in all the earth! You have set your glory above the heavens" (Psalm 8:1 NIV). "I trust in your unfailing love" (Psalm 13:5). David speaks of his commitment to declaring the name of God when he says, "I will declare your name to my people; in the assembly I will praise you" (Psalm 22:22 TNIV).

When you pray the name of God from God's Word, declaring and affirming who He is, the name of God and all its ramifications are inextricably woven in your heart.

When the Old Testament people of God made their declaration to God, their heart commitment influenced their relationship with the Lord, leading them to trust and obedience. Moses made this clear:

> You have today declared the LORD to be your God, and that you would walk in His ways and keep His statutes, His commandments and His ordinances, and listen to His voice. The LORD has today declared you to be His people, a treasured possession, as He promised you, and that you should keep all His commandments; and that He will set you high above all nations which He has made, for praise, fame, and honor; and that you shall be a consecrated people to the LORD your God, as He has spoken (Deuteronomy 26:17-19).

Your words of declaration about your God and to your God in His presence and in the presence of others are important both to you and to God. God takes you seriously when you speak with Him. And He loves to hear your declarations of who He is and how and why you trust in Him. You can make these declarations in three ways.

First, declare God's names to Him in prayer. When Hezekiah was in great trouble from his enemies, he spread his trouble out before the Lord and prayed, "O LORD, the God of Israel, who are enthroned above the cherubim, You are the God, You alone, of all the kingdoms of the earth. You have made heaven and earth. Incline Your ear, O LORD, and hear; open Your eyes, O LORD, and see" (2 Kings 19:15-16). God responded by saying, "I have heard you...I will defend this city to save it for My own sake and for My servant David's sake" (2 Kings 19:20,34). God responded to Hezekiah's request when Hezekiah declared the name of the Lord in prayer.

Next, declare the names of God to yourself—to your mind, heart, and soul. Jeremiah surely knew this great secret because he declared the names of God to his own mind: "This I recall to my mind, therefore I have hope. The LORD's lovingkindnesses indeed never cease, for His compassions never fail. They are new every morning; great is Your faithfulness" (Lamentations 3:21-23). Then Jeremiah spoke to his soul when he said, "'The LORD is my portion,' says my soul, 'therefore I have hope in Him'" (Lamentations 3:24). The sons of Korah declared, "Why are you downcast, O my soul? Why so disturbed within me? Put your hope in God, for I will yet praise him, my Savior and my God" (Psalm 42:11 NIV). When you speak the names of God to yourself, your heart will turn away from your fears and worries to a new courage and confidence in God.

Finally, declare the names of God to others. Peter says to "always be prepared to give an answer to everyone who asks you to give the reason for the hope that you have. But do this with gentleness and respect" (1 Peter 3:15 NIV). I love to tell others about God—who He is, what He does, and what He says. When you tell others about Him, you are declaring His name to them.

One morning I was having "breakfast with the Lord" at my favorite restaurant in Palm Desert, where I live. After I spent time with the Lord, I opened up my laptop to type some ideas for a new book. As a lady walked past, she stopped and turned to talk with me, asking what I was doing. I told her that I was writing some ideas for a book. She asked what kinds of books I write, and I told her that I write about God.

"Oh, I don't believe you can have a relationship with God," she said.

"Well, you're wrong," I replied. I'm not usually so blunt, but her statement was so matter-of-fact, and she was so certain of what she believed, the words just came out. I continued, "What if there is a God, and what if, more than anything, He does desire a relationship with you?"

She stood firm. "I don't believe it."

I pressed, "Do you know what God wants more than anything?"

"What?" she asked.

I said very simply, "You."

"What?" she asked again.

I said, "More than anything, God wants you."

She looked at me with a quizzical look on her face, and then emphatically said, "Well, that's why you're an author." Then she walked away. But I don't believe she'll ever forget our conversation. And I'm believing God to use our little exchange to melt away her misconceptions of God and bring her to a saving faith in Christ.

How can you declare God's names? The best way is to talk with God in prayer about what you have discovered as you have drawn near to Him.

These distinct declarations are your affirmations to God, yourself (mind, heart, and soul), and to others. You may even choose to write out a prayer in your journal or on the "Trusting in the Names of God" devotional Bible study pages for the *Quiet Time Notebook* (see appendix 2 for an example). Start with the words, "Lord, You are…" Then list everything you are learning about Him from His Word. I don't always write out my prayers, but I have found that when I do put prayers on paper, I more readily understand their spiritual significance. And remember that declaring the names of God brings honor to His name. One of the Ten Commandments instructs us to not take the Lord's name in vain (Exodus 20:7) because we are not to dishonor God's name in our speech or in our lives. Praying the names of God is a privilege.

Declaring the names of God is an integral part of my spiritual growth with the Lord. Recently, I received a phone call from my brother, telling me that my mother needed an emergency medical test. When I learned more about the test, I became alarmed. My mind immediately raced to the worst-case scenario, and I sank into a tremendous panic. I paced from one end of the house to the other, my anxiety increasing as I replayed the what-if script—*What if this happens?* and *What if that happens?* Suddenly, the Holy Spirit seemed to stop me in my tracks, and I began talking to myself. *Catherine, you are telling others about trusting in the names of God. What about you? What is it going to take for you to trust in the names of God in the middle of this situation? What do you know to be true about God?* Immediately I recited aloud everything I knew to be true about God. Then I prayed to my Lord, declaring His names and thanking Him for who I knew Him to be according to His Word. God's peace flooded my heart and calmed my soul. Declaring God's names to Him in prayer and to my mind, heart, and soul pulled me from a downward spiral into the blessed realm of trusting God.

Spurgeon speaks of the importance of linking your prayers with trust in God:

> Suppose you weep all night. Will that keep your ship from sinking? Suppose you could cry your eyes out. Will that make your employees honest? Suppose you could worry until you could not eat. Would that raise the value of your inventory? If

you were to say, "Well, I have done all that is to be done, and now I will leave it with God," one would think that you might have the full use of your senses to attend to your business and to get a good night's sleep. But you fritter away your senses and commit blunders that multiply your troubles, both in waking and sleeping. We say, "Leave good enough alone." I say to you, "Leave ill alone; leave them both alone." Then with the hand of prayer in everything, with thanksgiving, let your requests be made known to God (Phil. 4:6). Then with the other hand, the hand of faith, trust in the heavenly Father and lift the load off your shoulders and let the entire weight be left with your Eternal God. Cast your burden on the Lord.[1]

Joseph Scriven, an Irish-born Canadian theologian, received the news of his mother's serious illness. In his letter to his mother in about 1855, he included the following words, a declaration of trust in the name of Jesus. He wrote them solely for her comfort and not as a hymn:

What a Friend we have in Jesus, all our sins and griefs to bear!
What a privilege to carry everything to God in prayer!
O what peace we often forfeit, O what needless pain we bear,
All because we do not carry everything to God in prayer.

Have we trials and temptations? Is there trouble anywhere?
We should never be discouraged; take it to the Lord in prayer.
Can we find a friend so faithful who will all our sorrows share?
Jesus knows our every weakness; take it to the Lord in prayer.

Are we weak and heavy laden, cumbered with a load of care?
Precious Savior, still our refuge; take it to the Lord in prayer.
Do your friends despise, forsake you? Take it to the Lord in prayer!
In His arms He'll take and shield you; you will find a solace there.

My Response

DATE:

KEY VERSE: "I will declare your name to my people; in the assembly I will praise you" (Psalm 22:22 TNIV).

FOR FURTHER THOUGHT: How can you declare the name of God today? What do you need to say to yourself—to your mind, heart, and soul? Write a prayer to the Lord, expressing all that is on your heart today.

MY RESPONSE:

DEPEND ON HIS NAMES

*Some trust in chariots and some
in horses, but we trust in the
name of the LORD our God.*

PSALM 20:7 NIV

Depending on the names of God determines the stability and direction of your life. If your support is trustworthy with unlimited resources, you have a firm foundation. If your support is undependable without resources, you are on shaky ground indeed. David understood his own need for a dependable, trustworthy foundation when he said, "Some trust in chariots and some in horses, but we trust in the name of the LORD our God" (Psalm 20:7 NIV). The Amplified Bible says we will trust in and boast of the name of the Lord, whereas the NKJV says we will remember the name of the Lord. In present-day vernacular, we might say, "Some trust in money and some in position and possessions, but we depend on the name of our God."

Dependence on God's names requires yielding and surrendering our own control to God. We all wrestle with an inner need for control, as Paul explains in Romans 7:23: "In my inner being I delight in God's law; but I see another law at work in the members of my body, waging war against the law of my mind and making me a prisoner of the law of sin at work within my members." Paul urged the church to "offer your bodies as living sacrifices, holy and pleasing to God—this is your spiritual act of worship" (Romans 12:1 NIV).

Dependence on God means surrendering yourself, your loved ones, your circumstances, and your future to the only one who is trustworthy— God. This kind of unabashed surrender is not easy because trusting on a human level has taught us that people and things can disappoint us. But you can know that God is not like fallible human beings—He is good, perfect, loving, and faithful (Lamentations 3:22-25).

Sometimes the most innocuous events teach us about our dependence on God. One of my friends invited a group of us from women's ministries to Sedona to celebrate my birthday. She knew how much I loved the red rock country in Sedona and had organized surprises for us when we arrived. One of those surprises was a jeep ride—over open, rocky terrain with treacherous cliffs that fell hundreds of feet to the canyon floor.

I was instantly terrified. I did not like the idea of some unknown driver taking us straight up a rock cliff with only a piece of metal beneath us. I was ready to say, "No way. I am not doing this!" But as I turned to walk away, I met the driver of the jeep. He was a jovial young man who inspired confidence with his smile and excitement. I realized immediately that this man knew how to drive that jeep, he had driven on the roads many times, and he knew exactly how to maneuver the jeep up rocky passages and through winding, dangerous canyons.

As the jeep tour began, the driver was actually having fun, making jokes, and laughing. To my surprise, I was having as much fun as the driver, perhaps more confident than any of my traveling companions. This surprised me, and I pondered my unexpected response as we traveled in the jeep for the next hour. As you might guess, we all made it out alive. But do you know what I discovered? I discovered the great value of placing your trust in someone who is able and capable, who knows the road for the journey, and who has traveled it many times before you.

God is your driver in life. You can place your life in His hands, for He is capable, and He possesses unlimited resources. He created the universe, so He certainly possesses within Himself the ability to handle whatever comes your way. If He is able to create something out of nothing, He will be able to creatively take your life and weave a beautiful design for His glory. Trusting God, depending on Him, means you hand the keys of your life to Him and depend on Him to drive. Whenever you are tempted to take the wheel, just think of my jeep ride in Sedona. Sit back and leave the control in the hands of your Lord.

When God reveals Himself to you through His names, He will challenge you to trust Him in new ways so He can be the driver in your life. You may occasionally discover that a wrestling match ensues as you struggle to let go of areas in your life, relinquishing them to your Lord. Be encouraged and learn a lesson from Jacob's wrestling match. The choice to wrestle is never yours, but God's. That you are even wrestling is a sure sign of blessing ahead. God is leading you to a deeper knowledge of Him. You will learn in the wrestling that He is more than you thought He was—greater and more glorious than you had imagined.

Depending on the name of the Lord means you call out to Him when you are in need. You may be grieving a loss, the death of a dream, or a disastrous relationship. Whatever your circumstance, call out to your Lord. Calling on His name is your expression of trust in your time of need. We see in Genesis 4:26, following the murder of Abel, that "men began to call on the name of the LORD." When you begin to call on the name of your Lord, your newfound dependence on Him marks an important turning point in your life. The Hebrew word translated "call" is *qara,* and in this context it means to call on the name of God to summon His aid.[1] Calling on the name of God is the most common use of this word in the Old Testament and is usually associated with a critical or chronic need.[2] To call on the name of God is to assert and yield to His control and sovereignty in the circumstances of your life.

Psalm 116 shows the value of calling on the name of the Lord. The writer is experiencing overwhelming anguish and is "overcome by trouble and sorrow" (Psalm 116:3 NIV). But then he makes a decision. "Then I called on the name of the LORD: 'O LORD, save me!' " As a result of that prayer, the writer says, "The LORD is gracious and righteous; our God is full of compassion. The LORD protects the simplehearted; when I was in great need, he saved me. Be at rest once more, O my soul, for the LORD has been good to you" (Psalm 116:5-7 NIV).

When I was in such anguish over my mother's medical test and the possible outcome, it was only after I turned my thoughts to the names of God that I was able to cast my need on God, calling on Him to help us in our time of trouble. A supernatural peace flooded my heart. I realized that God was greater than my circumstance and perfectly capable of handling whatever came our way, regardless of the outcome. The test results were benign; none of my imagined worst-case scenarios came to fruition. And I learned the great value of trusting in the names of God.

God offers many promises to those who call out to Him. Some of my favorites include Psalm 34:6 (NIV), "This poor man called, and the LORD heard him; he saved him out of all his troubles," and Psalm 145:18 (NIV), "The LORD is near to all who call on him, to all who call on him in truth." Applying these promises to our lives by faith is the great requirement in trust. Jerry Bridges, author of *Trusting God,* explains:

> In order to trust God, we must always view our adverse circumstances through the eyes of faith, not of sense…faith to trust God in adversity comes through the Word of God alone. It is only in the Scriptures that we find an adequate view of God's relationship to and involvement in our painful circumstances. It is only from the Scriptures, applied to our hearts by the Holy Spirit, that we receive the grace to trust God in adversity.[3]

Octavius Winslow, a contemporary of Charles Spurgeon, said, "Faith is the spiritual spy of the soul. It travels far into the promised land, gathers the ripe clusters—the evidences and earnest of its reality and richness—and returning, bears with it these, the 'first-fruits' of the coming vintage."[4] The truths about God and His names, discovered in His Word, are great promises to find, embrace, trust, and live in your daily life.[5] Eagerly lay out your need before the Lord, and watch to see what He will accomplish. He is not worried or wondering how He can handle your circumstance. On the contrary, He has a plan and can masterfully weave the threads of your life into a masterpiece that brings Him glory.

How can we depend on God's names? You may choose to write a prayer in your journal or on the "Trusting in the Names of God" devotional Bible study pages for the *Quiet Time Notebook* (see appendix 2 for an example). Begin your prayer, "Lord, I need you because…" and then outline the nature of your needs. In essence, you are taking your hands off the wheel and turning the controls of your life over to your Lord. This decision requires a surrender of self and your need to control. It places your reliance on what you have discovered in God's Word about who He is and what He promises about Himself, His ways, and His works. You leave all the what-ifs behind and cast yourself entirely on the character and person of God Himself.

A story is told of a man who was lost and dying for a drink of water. He arrived at a weather-beaten old shack, where he found some shade. As he glanced around his new surroundings, he saw an old, rusty water pump nearby. He stumbled over to it, grabbed the handle, and began to pump up and down, up and down. Nothing came out. Disappointed, he staggered back to his resting place.

Then he noticed an old jug beside the shack. He wiped away the dirt and dust and read a message that said, "Prime the pump with all the water in this jug. Be sure to fill the jug again before you leave." He popped the cork out of the jug and discovered it was almost full of water! Suddenly, he was faced with a decision. If he drank the water, he could live, at least for a short amount of time. But if he poured all the water in the old rusty pump, maybe it would yield fresh, cool water from deep down in the well, all the water he could possibly want or need. He thought about both options. What should he do? Should he pour the jug of water into the old pump, possibly losing his opportunity for any refreshment, hoping for a chance on unending fresh, cool water? Or should he drink what was in the old jug and ignore its message? Should he spend all the water on the hopes of those instructions, which may have been written years ago?

Reluctantly he poured all the water into the pump. Then he grabbed the handle and began to pump. Nothing came out! He kept exerting pressure to the pump handle. A little bit began to dribble out, then a small stream, and finally it gushed! Much to his relief, fresh, cool water poured out. Eagerly, he filled the jug and drank from it. He filled it another time and once again drank its refreshing contents. Then he filled the jug for the next traveler. He filled it to the top, popped the cork back on, and added this little note: "Believe me, it really works. You have to give it all away before you can get anything back."

Hear the lesson from this weary traveler who counted on and acted on the words of the instructions as the answer for his deepest need. The Bible is filled with tremendous promises about your God, all wrapped up in His names. You can depend on God as the great solution to all you face today. Turn to Him. Call on His name. Hand the keys of your life to Him and depend on Him. Then watch to see what He will do.

He Shall Not Fail

He shall not fail, nor shall He be discouraged,
Though all things earthly in ruin shall blend;
Infinite power and infinite patience,
From the beginning He seeth the end.
Let us trust in Him, work with Him, wait for Him
Though long the days and the visions all fail,
Though our faint hearts grow despondent and fearful,
Though naught our strength and efforts avail;
Forces of evil sweep onward exultant,
Even the faithful seem conquered at length;
Let us hold fast to this rock of assurance,
Let us find peace in this tower of strength.
"He fainteth not and He groweth not weary,"
All ye that labor this comfort may take;
Be of good courage, He goeth before thee,
He shall not fail thee, nor shall He forsake.
Let us walk with Him, lean on Him, cling to Him
He will uphold e'en the weakest that live;
Glory to God! For with strength He doth gird us,
Power and might to the faint He doth give;
Here in this bulwark our faith finds a refuge,
Ne'er may we measure its breadth and its length;
When all the arms that we leaned on have failed us,
Praises to Him, for His joy is our strength.[6]

ANNIE JOHNSON FLINT

DATE:

KEY VERSE: "Some trust in chariots and some in horses, but we trust in the name of the LORD our God" (Psalm 20:7 NIV).

FOR FURTHER THOUGHT: In what ways do you need to depend on the names of God and call on Him today? Where in your life do you need to let go of the wheel, relinquishing control to Him? Write a prayer to your Lord, expressing all that is on your heart. Begin with the words, "Lord, I need You because…"

MY RESPONSE:

Day Eleven

DELIGHT IN
HIS NAMES

I will be glad and rejoice in you;
I will sing the praises of your name, O Most High.

PSALM 9:2 TNIV

When you experience God through His names, you will praise and worship Him. David expressed his delight in the names of God again and again as he discovered, drew near to, declared, and depended on the names of God. He said, "I will be glad and rejoice in you; I will sing the praises of your name, O Most High" (Psalm 9:2 TNIV).

Do you delight in the Lord? You cannot find delight in Him if you do not know Him. Dick Eastman, in his book *A Celebration of Praise,* offers the key to praise. He says, "Effective praise has its focus on our Lord alone. The more we are able to focus our praises exclusively on the nature and character of God the Father, the Son, and the Holy Spirit, the more power we will experience as the result of that praise."[1]

Knowing God's names is the great secret to a life of praise and worship. Darlene Zschech, the writer of the great worship song "Shout to the Lord" says, "No matter what you are facing, your answer is in the arms of God.

Psalm 138:2 says, 'I will bow down toward your holy temple and will praise your name for your love and your faithfulness, for you have exalted above all things your name and your word.'" She continues, "God is exalted above anything that you face—above any disappointment, above any brokenness, above anything that tries to exalt itself higher than the name of Jesus. He has promised us His name and His Word."[2] Your worship and delight is filled with the magnificent facts discovered in God's Word about God Himself.

Darlene is part of the Hillsong Australia worship team and is one of the most awe-inspiring worship leaders I've ever had the privilege to watch. Just to see her face looking toward heaven fills one with a greater desire to know and love the Lord. Darlene describes her perspective of worship:

> To worship is to speak *to the Lord* with words full of adoration. To worship God is to bow down to Him, to revere Him, and to hold in awe His beauty. I see worship as a kiss toward heaven. Worship is a verb, defined as "regard with great or extravagant respect, honor, or devotion." It is an active expression of our love toward God. It is vibrant and visible by our deeds and not only by the words we speak. Worship involves the giving of ourselves totally to the Lord. Worship is neither a ritualistic activity nor a musical emotion. It embodies and reflects the selfless generosity of Christ. Worship is a movement of our hearts, our thoughts, and our wills toward God's heart, thoughts, and will.[3]

Augustine viewed worship as a celebration. "In the house of God there is never-ending festival; the angel choir makes eternal holiday; the presence of God's face gives joy that never fails. And from that everlasting, perpetual festivity there sounds in the ears of the heart a strain, mysterious, melodious, sweet—provided the world does not drown it."[4] I define worship as "overwhelming delight in God." David said, "Delight yourself in the LORD and he will give you the desires of your heart" (Psalm 37:4 NIV). The Hebrew word translated "delight yourself" is *anag* and means to be happy about and take exquisite delight in God. Delighting in God does not necessarily result in receiving what you wanted or hoped for. God takes your own minuscule desires and often enlarges your heart to a new size capable of holding a new vision of His plans and purposes. The psalmist said, "I shall run the way of

Your commandments, for You will enlarge my heart" (Psalm 119:32). You will notice that your delight in God often results in new, greater desires than you previously held in your heart.

When you delight in God, your awe of what you have seen of Him in the discovery of His names will sometimes cause you to fall on your face before Him. Moses "bowed to the ground at once and worshiped" (Exodus 34:8 NIV) when he saw God passing in front of him. When Isaiah saw God as "the LORD Almighty," he cried out, "Woe to me…for I am a man of unclean lips, and I live among a people of unclean lips, and my eyes have seen the King, the LORD Almighty" (Isaiah 6:5 TNIV). When John saw the glorified revelation of Jesus on the isle of Patmos, he "fell at his feet as though dead" (Revelation 1:17 NIV).

Make no mistake, dear friend, when you truly "see" God as you discover His names, draw near to His names, declare His names, and depend on His names, your vision of God will be such that your overwhelming thrill and delight will likely drive you to your knees and even down on your face before Him. My mother, who is battling multiple sclerosis, remarks that one of her greatest challenges is that she cannot any longer fall to her knees to worship. She sits in a wheelchair, but her heart is bowed in worship and adoration of her Lord.

How can we delight in God's names? Delighting in the names of God is the result of trusting in God. To delight in His name, you may wish to write a prayer to the Lord in your journal or on the "Trusting in the Names of God" devotional Bible study pages for the *Quiet Time Notebook* (see appendix 2 or figure 3 for an example). Begin with "Lord, I love You because…" You may want to praise and worship the Lord using a hymnbook or worship music. Take time to celebrate the magnificent beauty of your Lord. When you delight and appreciate His beauty, He is not the only one who appreciates your love for Him. Others will take notice of your delight in God.

I was staying at a small hotel in Camarillo, California, where I like to retreat to write my books. One evening at dusk, I noticed a particularly beautiful sunset. Ever the photographer, I grabbed my digital camera and ran out to the parking lot, eager to catch the colorful beauty of the sky, the clouds, and the sun. I stood still in the center of the lot, snapping one picture after another. Cars pulled up, parked, and people got out. Instead of going into the hotel, people walked over to where I was standing and looked in the direction of my camera. Only then did they see what had captured my attention—the magnificent display of God, His signature on His handiwork, in the sunset. One man said, "You're trying to catch the sunset, aren't you?" All eyes were on God's event of the sunset that evening. And so it is when you worship and delight in God. Others turn their eyes to look at where you are focused. Your worship, delight, and praise helps those around you see a new view of God, moving their eyes from the earth to look up to heaven and see what they have never seen before.

Delighting in God amplifies the spiritual things of God and discounts the importance of the temporal, earthly life that will soon be past. We must learn to keep our eyes focused on the eternal in the midst of the temporal. Paul said, "So we fix our eyes not on what is seen, but on what is unseen. For what is seen is temporary, but what is unseen is eternal" (2 Corinthians 4:18 NIV). Trusting in the names of God is how we fix our eyes on the unseen and eternal things, resulting in overwhelming delight in God.

Trusting in the Names of God

Those who know Your name will put their trust in You.
Psalm 9:10

Declare His Name

LORD, YOU ARE...

my creator and the Triune God. You created all things, the earth, the universe, and even me. You are the Triune God: the Father, the Son, and the Holy Spirit.

Depend on His Name

LORD, I NEED YOU BECAUSE...

of a current impossible situation. Elohim, You are Creator, and You can do anything. You can breathe life into this difficulty. I lay it before You now and I ask You to work out something only You can do.

Delight in His Name

LORD, I LOVE YOU BECAUSE...

You are majestic, eternal, all-powerful, and greater than anything I face today. I love You because You created me, my incredible family, and my friends. You are the Master Designer, who did the most amazing design of the universe and the human body. I love how You chose green for trees and blue for sky. You are perfection and infinite beauty.

FIGURE 3

My Response

DATE:

KEY VERSE: "I will be glad and rejoice in you; I will sing the praises of your name, O Most High" (Psalm 9:2 TNIV).

FOR FURTHER THOUGHT: As you think about all you have learned this week, take some time now to write a prayer to the Lord, delighting in Him. Begin your prayer with, "Lord, I love You because…"

MY RESPONSE:

Day Twelve

QUIET TIME WEEK TWO: TRUSTING IN GOD'S NAMES

They entered into a covenant to seek the LORD, the God of their fathers, with all their heart and soul.

2 CHRONICLES 15:12 NIV

PREPARE YOUR HEART

In the last two weeks you have had the opportunity to think about the great adventure of knowing God and trusting in Him. The Bible, from cover to cover, is filled with living examples of men and women who discovered God, drew near to Him, declared His name, depended on His name, and ultimately delighted in Him. King Asa is one of those great examples. And yet every man or woman of God has great feet of clay, including Asa, who sometimes acted foolishly and relied on the strength of men instead of God. Following one of his failures, the word of the Lord came to Asa: "Were not the Ethiopians and the Lubim an immense army with very many chariots and horsemen? Yet because you relied on the LORD, He delivered them into your hand. For the eyes of the LORD move to and fro throughout the earth that He may strongly support those whose heart is completely His" (2 Chronicles 16:8-9).

Think, dear friend, about the truth of those words. God's eyes are indeed moving to and fro throughout the earth looking...looking...looking for hearts committed to Him, for hearts that will rely on Him. Will you draw near to the Lord and ask Him to give you that kind of heart? Ask God to quiet your heart and speak to you from His Word today.

READ AND STUDY GOD'S WORD

1. Last week in your quiet time, you had the opportunity to read King Asa's prayer in the heat of the battle in 2 Chronicles 14:11. In his prayer, he spoke of his reliance on God, and God saved him out of his trouble. Following that event, God's word came to Asa, saying, "Be strong and do not give up, for your work will be rewarded" (2 Chronicles 15:7 TNIV).

Read 2 Chronicles 15:7-12 and write out what you learn about King Asa's response to the word of God:

2. In what way does Asa's response show his trust in the names of God?

3. The Hebrew for "took courage" is *chazaq* and means to make firm, to hold fast, to be strong, courageous, and valiant. What was Asa holding fast to?

4. The Bible speaks often about trusting God. Look at the following verses and write what you learn about trust in God. Personalize each of your insights and observations. For example, "If I know God's name, I will trust in Him (from Psalm 9:10).

Psalm 9:10

Psalm 20:7 ("Boast" in the NASB is "trust" in the NIV.)

Psalm 22:4-5

Psalm 31:14

Psalm 33:21

Psalm 37:3-7

Isaiah 50:10

Jeremiah 17:5-8

Zephaniah 3:12 ("Take refuge" in the NASB is also translated "trust" in the NIV.)

5. Describe in your own words what it means to trust in the names of God.

ADORE GOD IN PRAYER

Talk with the Lord today about those areas in your life where you have difficulty trusting Him. Will you, as Peter encourages, "cast all your anxiety on him because he cares for you" (1 Peter 5:7 NIV)?

If I really trust Him,
Shall I ever fret?
If I really do expect Him,
Can I e'er forget?
If by faith I really see Him,
Shall I doubt His aid?
If I really love Him,
Can I be afraid?[1]

YIELD YOURSELF TO GOD

To know God's name is to know Him in an intimate personal way. It is more than just knowing facts about God. It is coming into a deeper personal relationship with Him as a result of seeking Him in the midst of our personal pain and discovering Him to be trustworthy. It is only as we know God in this personal way that we come to trust Him.[2]

JERRY BRIDGES

ENJOY HIS PRESENCE

How do you need to take courage in the Lord today and trust in Him? Will you take time now to enter into a commitment, following the example of the people of Israel, to seek the Lord with all your heart and soul? Write your prayer of commitment and trust in the space provided.

REST IN HIS LOVE

"Who is among you that fears the LORD, that obeys the voice of His servant, that walks in darkness and has no light? Let him trust in the name of the LORD and rely on his God" (Isaiah 50:10).

Week Three

DISCOVERING GOD'S
GREATNESS AND GLORY

Days 13–18

TRUSTING IN ELOHIM—HE IS YOUR CREATOR

*In the beginning God created
the heavens and the earth.*

GENESIS 1:1

rusting in Elohim answers the most profound questions of life. Who am I? Why am I here? What is my purpose? God answers these questions in the very first chapter of the Bible, Genesis 1. He begins the Bible with the signature of His name *Elohim* in the very first words: "In the beginning God created the heavens and the earth" (Genesis 1:1). He proceeds to explain that He, Elohim, created not only the heavens and the earth but also man: "In the image of God He created him; male and female He created them" (Genesis 1:27). In these words we see the origin of life—God Himself. Who is this God? He is, according to the first chapter of Genesis, Elohim. Do you long to understand who you are, why you are here, and what your purpose is in life? Run to Elohim.

DISCOVER ELOHIM

The Hebrew word translated "God" in Genesis 1:1 is *Elohim* and means "God, the one true God," with the root *El* referring to "mighty one, strength."[1] Its plural construction points to the triune nature of God. The first and preeminent name of God, *Elohim* stresses God's might, power, majesty, and omnipotence, and is called by Henry Morris the "mighty name of God, the Creator."[2] *Elohim* occurs more than 2000 times in the Bible and 35 times in Genesis 1:1–2:3 alone in connection with His creative power. This name of God is found most frequently in Deuteronomy and Psalms.

DRAW NEAR TO ELOHIM

Why would God begin His revelation to us with this name? Genesis is the book of beginnings, and Elohim, self-existent and eternal, is the author of all beginnings. He is outside the realm of time, wholly other and infinite. And yet, profoundly and intensely personal, He has chosen to create. The name *Elohim* reveals much about God.

In the plural construction of His name, we see Elohim is a mystery, for He is triune—one in three—Father, Son, and Holy Spirit. When you contemplate God, you step onto the ground of the incomprehensible, gaze at the majestic Godhead, and contemplate what you cannot wrap your mind around. In short, you are in the territory of what Tozer calls "mystery": "We cover our deep ignorance with words, but we are ashamed to wonder, we are afraid to whisper 'mystery.' "[3] Do not be afraid, dear friend. Venture onward into the vast, unfathomable land of God and look with awe and wonder.

The name *Elohim* is in plural form, yet it is paired with singular verbs and adjectives throughout Scripture. The one true God even refers to Himself using plural pronouns: "Let Us make man in Our image, in Our likeness" (Genesis 1:26). "The man has become like one of Us" (Genesis 3:22). "Come, let Us go down there and confuse their language, so that they will not understand one another's speech" (Genesis 11:7). Clearly God is our one true God, as seen in Deuteronomy 10:17 (NIV): "For the LORD your God is God [Elohim] of gods and Lord of lords, the great God, mighty and awesome, who shows no partiality and accepts no bribes." And yet, according to the Bible, He is triune—we see the three persons of the Trinity functioning together. "And now the Lord God has sent Me, and His Spirit" (Isaiah 48:16). We see the Trinity involved in creation: "God [Elohim] created the heavens and the earth" (Genesis 1:1). "The Spirit of God was moving over the surface of the waters" (Genesis 1:2). "He was in the world, and the world was made through Him" (John 1:10, referring to Jesus).

So Elohim is triune, and He is the Creator. Herbert Lockyer says that in Elohim, "God is the majestic Ruler, and under such a name we have the idea of omnipotence, or creative and governing power."[4] Nathan Stone, author of *The Names of God,* says that as Elohim is possessor and ruler of heaven and earth, His presence cannot be confined by space, his power does not require man's help, and through "His great will and power and agency all things and nations have their being."[5]

Elohim created the heavens and the earth, and even more profoundly, He created you. What does knowing Elohim tell you about yourself? You are created, and because God created you, you have personal worth and significance. God is the Giver of life, and He has given you life. Knowing you are created in the image of God for His glory answers a thousand questions in your life. You can know, because you are created in the image of God, that God has attached an intrinsic value and worth to you, regardless of how you may feel about yourself.

Psalm 139:13-16 reveals the intimate details of your creation: "I am fearfully and wonderfully made…my frame was not hidden from You, when I was made in secret…your eyes have seen my unformed substance." Because God designed you, He has attached a high value to you, even thinking about and planning your days on earth in advance (Psalm 139:16). He has created you for a purpose—for His glory. "Bring…everyone who is called by My name, and whom I have created for My glory, whom I have formed, even whom I have made" (Isaiah 43:7).

What does it mean to be created for God's glory? The Hebrew word translated "glory" is *kabod* and refers to the splendor of God's presence. Your life is meant to show the greatness and glory and, in fact, the very presence and existence of God. When you trust in Elohim, relying on Him, your life becomes the platform where He displays His magnificence. Jesus says your light is to "shine before others, that they may see your good deeds and glorify your Father in heaven" (Matthew 5:16 TNIV). Paul confirms this purpose when he says that you will shine in the world "like stars in the sky as you hold firmly to the word of life" (Philippians 2:15-16 TNIV). Your life, lived for Elohim's glory, demonstrates His very existence to the world around you.

Trusting Jesus as Creator

"But of the Son He says, 'Your throne, O God, is forever and ever, and the righteous scepter is the scepter of His kingdom'" (Hebrews 1:8).

The writer of Hebrews is declaring that God's words in Psalm 45:6 are referring to Jesus, the Son. He is making clear that God Himself refers to Jesus as Elohim in Psalm 45:6 and declares He has an eternal throne. Jesus, as the second person of the Triune God, is eternal and self-existent, and He was involved in the act of creation (John 1:1-12).

DECLARE ELOHIM

When you are questioning the reality of God or His nearness, open your front door, walk outside, and look at God's creation. Look up at the sky, look out at the birds, trees, and fields, and look down at the intricacy of your hand. Then declare, *Elohim, You created the heavens and the earth, and You have made me in Your image.* When you find yourself in an impossible situation, call out to Elohim with the words of the psalmist: "I will say to the LORD, 'My refuge and my fortress, my God [Elohim], in whom I trust'" (Psalm 91:2). Speak to your own mind, heart, and soul, "The Everlasting God, the LORD, the Creator of the ends of the earth does not become weary or tired. His understanding is inscrutable. He gives strength to the weary, and to him who lacks might He increases power" (Isaiah 40:28-29). Then, when others doubt the presence, power, and person of God, tell them about Elohim, that "the LORD your God is the God of gods and the Lord of lords, the great, the mighty, and the awesome God" (Deuteronomy 10:17).

DEPEND ON ELOHIM

Imagine God flinging the stars out in the universe and speaking planets into existence. Think about Him forming a human being from the dust of the earth, breathing life into His creation. Then contemplate His ability to breathe life into your impossible circumstance, whatever it may be. God, the uncreated, eternal, all-powerful, mighty, and majestic Creator, is greater than any obstacle you face today. You can rely on Him, the Designer of the universe and the human body, to weave a design into your life even when your circumstances may seem to be as formless and empty as the earth was prior to the completion of Elohim's work. What must you do in response? You owe Him your very life. Give Him your greatest allegiance, your deepest devotion, and your highest service.

Ethel Waters was born to a woman who was raped at the age of 12. What could Elohim possibly do with one such as Ethel Waters, seemingly a mistake, the result of a brutal attack? What was Elohim's plan? One talent set her apart from many others—she could sing. She performed for the first time at the age of five in a church program. Reared in poverty, she left school at the age of 13 to support herself as a maid. She performed on the vaudeville circuit, moved to New York City, and recorded songs for various record labels. Eventually she played singing roles in Broadway productions and starred in nine films between 1929 and 1959, even receiving an Academy Award nomination as best supporting actress in *Pinky* (1949).

Something else set her apart from others in her day—she loved God. Her God, Elohim, opened a wonderful door for her in life and gave her the privilege of touring with evangelist Billy Graham from 1957 to 1976. Anyone who ever heard her sing will never forget her amazing rendition of "His Eye Is on the Sparrow." Her dependence on and knowledge of Elohim were evident when she sang those words:

> "Let not your heart be troubled," His tender word I hear,
> And resting on His goodness, I lose my doubts and fears;
> Though by the path He leadeth, but one step I may see;
> His eye is on the sparrow, and I know He watches me;
> His eye is on the sparrow, and I know He watches me.
>
> I sing because I'm happy,
> I sing because I'm free,

For His eye is on the sparrow,
And I know He watches me.[6]

Others may have thought Ethel Waters was a mistake, looking only at her humble beginnings. But Ethel Waters knew Elohim and remained confident she was on earth by His design. And you can know the same truth. You are God's design. Draw near to Elohim today and depend on Him to weave His design into your life.

DELIGHT IN ELOHIM

How can you delight in Elohim today? Think about His power in creation, which He specifically outlined in Job 38–42 when He addressed Job: "Where were you when I laid the earth's foundation?…I made the clouds its garment and wrapped it in thick darkness, when I fixed limits for it and set its doors and bars in place…Have you ever given orders to the morning, or shown the dawn its place?…Who has the wisdom to count the clouds? Who can tip over the water jars of heaven?" (Job 38:4,9-10,12,37 NIV).

Imagine Elohim sitting "enthroned above the circle of the earth" as He "stretches out the heavens like a canopy" (Isaiah 40:22 NIV). Listen to His promise when you are afraid: "Do not fear, for I am with you; do not anxiously look about you, for I am your God. I will strengthen you, surely I will help you, surely I will uphold you with My righteous right hand" (Isaiah 41:10).

And finally, think about His greatness and glory, seen in His triune nature—the Father, the Son, and the Holy Spirit. When Isaiah saw the Lord, He was "seated on a throne, high and exalted, and the train of his robe filled the temple" (Isaiah 6:1 NIV). Heavenly creatures (seraphim) flew above Him and called, not once but three times (perhaps referring to the Trinity), "Holy, holy, holy is the LORD Almighty; the whole earth is full of his glory." Fall on your face, dear friend, and worship your Elohim.

Holy, holy, holy! Lord God Almighty!
Early in the morning our song shall rise to Thee;
Holy, holy, holy, merciful and mighty!
God in three persons, blessed Trinity!

Holy, holy, holy! All the saints adore Thee,
Casting down their golden crowns around the glassy sea;
Cherubim and seraphim falling down before Thee,
Who was, and is, and evermore shall be.

Holy, holy, holy! though the darkness hide Thee,
Though the eye of sinful man Thy glory may not see;
Only Thou art holy; there is none beside Thee,
Perfect in power, in love, and purity.

Holy, holy, holy! Lord God Almighty!
All Thy works shall praise Thy name, in earth, and sky, and sea;
Holy, holy, holy; merciful and mighty!
God in three persons, blessed Trinity!

REGINALD HEBER

My Response

DATE:

KEY VERSE: "In the beginning God created the heavens and the earth" (Genesis 1:1).

FOR FURTHER THOUGHT: What is the most important truth you learned about Elohim? Write a prayer to Elohim, expressing all that is on your heart. (As you read about God's names, you may want to summarize what you learn on the "Trusting in the Names of God" worksheet in appendix 2 by writing out each Hebrew name, English name, meaning, and related Scripture.)

MY RESPONSE:

Day Fourteen

TRUSTING IN EL ELYON—HE IS YOUR SOVEREIGN

Blessed be Abram of God Most High,
possessor of heaven and earth; and
blessed be God Most High, who has
delivered your enemies into your hand.

GENESIS 14:19-20

To trust in El Elyon is to know who is in control of your life. El Elyon reveals He is sovereign, He is in control, and He rules over all things. Abram first discovered God as El Elyon from the words of Melchizedek, priest of God Most High: "Blessed be Abram of God Most High, possessor of heaven and earth; and blessed be God Most High, who has delivered your enemies into your hand" (Genesis 14:19-20). Who is the one you can count on when everyone and everything seems to be working against you? Who is in charge of your life? His name is El Elyon.

Discover El Elyon

The Hebrew words translated "God Most High" are *El Elyon* and mean elevated, high, exalted—the Supreme Being (the true God).[1] Henry Morris, founder of Institute for Creation Research, says the revelation of El Elyon stressed "the absolute superiority of God to the multitude of gods and goddesses worshiped in Canaan."[2] El Elyon is introduced into the life experience of Abram, who later was renamed Abraham by God Himself. The name *El Elyon* occurs 4 times in Genesis 14:18-22 and approximately 40 times throughout the Old Testament, including 20 times in Psalms and 12 times in Daniel.

Draw Near to El Elyon

God revealed Himself as El Elyon to Abram following Abram's great victory over enemy kings from Chaldea and Persia (Genesis 14). During the war of the kings, Abram's nephew, Lot, had been taken captive. When Abram heard about his nephew's plight, he and his men attacked the kings, defeated them, and recovered all of Lot's possessions, returning Lot and his family to safety. But the story does not end there. Following such a great victory, Abram was approached by two kings, the king of Sodom and Melchizedek, the king of Salem. Melchizedek, a worshipper of the true God, brought Abram bread and wine (gifts) and blessed him, saying, "Blessed be Abram of God Most High [El Elyon], possessor of heaven and earth. And blessed be God Most High [El Elyon], who delivered your enemies into your hand."

In stark contrast, the king of Sodom attempted to bribe Abram. "Give me the people and keep the goods for yourself" (Genesis 14:21 NIV). Abram was suddenly faced with a choice of trust, belief, and perspective. Would he live his life as a self-reliant man or a God-reliant man? Was he the one who had gained the victory over the enemy kings, or was El Elyon the provider of victory, as Melchizedek had declared?

Abram wasted no words in his response to the king of Sodom. "I have raised my hand to the LORD, God Most High, Creator of heaven and earth, and have taken an oath that I will accept nothing belonging to you, not even a thread or the thong of a sandal, so that you will never be able to say, 'I made Abram rich'" (Genesis 14:23 NIV). What a man of faith! Abram knew El Elyon as his God, sovereign and supreme over every detail of his life. For him there was no choice between earthly reliance and God-reliance; Abram chose to rely on God. Herbert Lockyer says that this new revelation of El Elyon was a "red letter day in the life of Abram in that it immediately brought him into a new closeness of relationship with His Lord."[3] It will be a red letter day for you as well when you discover, draw near to, and depend on El Elyon.

Over and over again in your life, you will return to the acknowledgement of El Elyon as sovereign. As you are faced with difficulties or challenges, you will be tempted to believe in chance and attribute circumstances to luck. That's what the world would have you believe. I have a belt that has little silver hearts on it, each with a different word written on it: *faith, hope, love, trust,* and the like. One evening when I happened to be wearing that belt, two women walked up to me and began reading the words on my belt. They came to a word on one of the hearts that I've never liked: *luck.*

"I don't believe in luck," I said.

"No, we don't either!" they replied.

After that, I decided I wouldn't wear the belt again until I removed all the hearts that said *luck.* I never even open fortune cookies—you know why? I don't believe in reading a fortune and thinking it has anything to say to me. I don't read astrology because I don't believe in astrological forecasts. I read the Bible and believe what God says. And I believe He is the one who rules.

Joseph, the elder of the two sons of Jacob by Rachel, came to know the power of El Elyon when he was a mere slave at the seat of Egyptian political power. As if being sold into slavery by his brothers were not enough, he was wrongly accused of accosting his master's wife and thrown into jail. Yet the Bible tells us that "the LORD was with Joseph and extended kindness to him, and gave him favor in the sight of the chief jailer…the LORD was with him; and whatever he did, the LORD made to prosper" (Genesis 39:21-23). Miraculously, El Elyon empowered Joseph to interpret dreams, first for his fellow prisoners and ultimately for Pharaoh himself. Pharaoh ascribed the interpretive power to Joseph: "When you hear a dream, you can interpret it." But Joseph trusted El Elyon and responded, "It is not in me; God will give Pharaoh a favorable answer."

Pharaoh released Joseph from jail and made him the ruler of Egypt, second only to Pharaoh. And according to the interpretation of Pharaoh's dream, seven years of plenty were followed by seven years of famine. As a result of the famine, Joseph's brothers came from the land of Canaan to Egypt to buy grain. At first, they did not recognize their brother, but Joseph recognized them. When Joseph finally revealed himself to his brothers, they were terrified because of what they had done to him. Listen to Joseph's words and consider your own response to adversity when you must trust that El Elyon is at work in your life: "Now do not be grieved or angry with yourselves, because you sold me here, for God sent me before you to preserve life…Now therefore, it was not you who sent me here, but God; and He has made me a father to Pharaoh and lord of all his household and ruler over all the land of Egypt" (Genesis 45:5-8).

Do you hear what Joseph is saying? God is ultimately the One who is in control, and all of man's actions play into His hands. People may intend great evil toward us. And we, in fact, may make grievous mistakes and fail. But God is greater than those who intend evil: "Greater is He who is in us than he who is in the world." And God, in fact, is greater than our failing hearts because "God causes all things to work together for good to those who love God and are called according to His purpose" (Romans 8:28).

What does knowing El Elyon tell you about yourself? You are not in control; El Elyon is in control. Overwhelming victory comes from El Elyon. Abram and Joseph both learned to trust El Elyon as the one who gave them victory in the heat of the battle (Genesis 14:19-20). But this victory is not for biblical saints alone. You can emerge victorious in the battles you face, for Paul tells us that we are "more than conquerors through him who loved us" (Romans 8:37 NIV).

Trusting Jesus as Sovereign

"For we were not following cleverly devised stories when we made known to you the power and coming of our Lord Jesus Christ (the Messiah), but we were eyewitnesses of His majesty (grandeur, authority of sovereign power)" (2 Peter 1:16 AMP).

In the context of El Elyon's rule, He has exercised His divine prerogative and sacrificed His Son to pay for our sins that we might be redeemed and saved. The sacrifice of Jesus is the proof of His amazing love. And we are told that nothing can ever separate us from His love

(Romans 8:38-39). His sovereignty is a mystery, and yet we know that within His control, we have the opportunity for salvation through Jesus Christ, that He does not want anyone to perish. We also know that "as many as received Him, to them He gave the right to become children of God, even to those who believe in His name" (John 1:12).

DECLARE EL ELYON

When you are doubting the sovereignty and rule of God in your life, take your worries to the Lord and offer the prayer of David to your El Elyon:

> Yours, O LORD, is the greatness and the power and the glory and the victory and the majesty, indeed everything that is in the heavens and the earth; Yours is the dominion, O LORD, and You exalt Yourself as head over all. Both riches and honor come from You, and You rule over all, and in Your hand is power and might; and it lies in Your hand to make great and to strengthen everyone (1 Chronicles 29:11-12).

And when you are discouraged about the answers for your life, speak to your own mind, heart, and soul, "I will cry to God Most High [El Elyon], to God who accomplishes all things for me" (Psalm 57:2).

When those around you question the works and ways of God, declare the ways of El Elyon in Daniel 4:34-35 (NIV): "His dominion is an eternal dominion; his kingdom endures from generation to generation. All the peoples of the earth are regarded as nothing. He does as he pleases with the powers of heaven and the peoples of the earth. No one can hold back his hand or say to him: 'What have you done?'" May your life declare that "the LORD Most High is to be feared, a great King over all the earth" (Psalm 47:2).

DEPEND ON HIS NAME

Do you have a problem with current events in your life? Are people around you causing great trouble? Is your financial situation a complete disaster? Your wisest response is to take all your troubles to El Elyon, God Most High, ruler of all things. Most people spend days, months, and sometimes even years complaining about their plight. El Elyon possesses within Himself the power and might to change people, events, and circumstances right now and in the future. I am not endorsing a "name it and claim it" philosophy, where we would presume to tell God what He should do and when He should do it. But I am advocating that whatever the scope of your troubles, you can take them to El Elyon and then watch, wait, and see what He will do in His perfect time.

Do not be surprised if the greatest change takes place right inside of you—how you think and how you walk with God. But then again, when you run to El Elyon with your problems, you can be assured that you are going to see something happen because El Elyon is the God who makes things happen! Sometimes He will deliver you as He did when He delivered Lot. Sometimes He will use you in a surprisingly powerful way in your present circumstances, giving you strength and wisdom as He did with Joseph. And sometimes He will dramatically change the course of your life as He did in the case of Abraham when He called him to leave everything and travel to an unknown country.

I had been agonizing about two difficult situations that had overwhelmed me for three or four years. Finally, one day, at my wits' end, I took these two situations to El Elyon and prayed some very specific requests, asking Him to do something about my troubles. Within a week, two dramatic events occurred, changing both those prolonged difficulties for the better. I will never forget what God accomplished, and I learned something powerful about El Elyon.

If you have a problem with the way things are going in your life, take it up with the Lord. There is no help in complaining to everyone around you. There is no victory in giving up. Running to El Elyon and trusting Him is the way to find your answer. Remember, He can change hearts. He can thwart difficult people. He can find new jobs. El Elyon is sovereign and in control.

Adelaide Pollard wanted more than anything else to go to Africa and serve the Lord as a missionary. However, she was unable to raise the necessary funds for the trip. Disappointed and brokenhearted, she attended a prayer meeting. During the time of prayer, a woman prayed, "It's all right,

Lord. It doesn't matter what you bring into our lives. Just have your own way with us." Adelaide went home that night with a new perspective, and as a result, she wrote one of the most beloved hymns of all time, "Have Thine Own Way." She trusted the name of El Elyon and realized He was the potter and she was the clay (Romans 9:20-21).

DELIGHT IN EL ELYON

Think about the power and protection of El Elyon in the words of Psalm 91:1-2 (NIV): "He who dwells in the shelter of the Most High will rest in the shadow of the Almighty. I will say of the LORD, 'He is my refuge and my fortress, my God, in whom I trust.'" Resolve to live your life in the light of El Elyon, your sovereign God, who is supreme over all. "Let them know that you, whose name is the LORD—that you alone are the Most High over all the earth" (Psalm 83:18 NIV). Rejoice in El Elyon as greater than any challenge you face in life today, remembering the psalmist's words: "For You are the LORD Most High over all the earth; You are exalted far above all gods" (Psalm 97:9).

> Have Thine own way, Lord! Have Thine own way!
> Thou art the potter, I am the clay.
> Mold me and make me after Thy will,
> While I am waiting, yielded and still.
>
> Have Thine own way, Lord! Have Thine own way!
> Search me and try me, Master, today!
> Whiter than snow, Lord, wash me just now,
> As in Thy presence humbly I bow.
>
> Have Thine own way, Lord! Have Thine own way!
> Wounded and weary, help me, I pray!
> Power, all power, surely is Thine!
> Touch me and heal me, Savior divine!
>
> Have Thine own way, Lord! Have Thine own way!
> Hold o'er my being absolute sway.
> Fill with Thy Spirit till all shall see
> Christ only, always, living in me!
>
> ADELAIDE A. POLLARD

My Response

DATE:

KEY VERSE: "Blessed be Abram of God Most High, possessor of heaven and earth; and blessed be God Most High, who has delivered your enemies into your hand" (Genesis 14:19-20).

FOR FURTHER THOUGHT: What did you learn from the example of Abram and his discovery of El Elyon? In what way do you need El Elyon in your life today? What describes you more—self-reliant or God-reliant? Where in your life do you need to be more reliant on El Elyon?

MY RESPONSE:

Day Fifteen

TRUSTING IN ADONAI—HE IS YOUR LORD

"Do not fear, Abram, I am a shield to you; your reward shall be very great." Abram said, "O Lord GOD, what will You give me, since I am childless?"

GENESIS 15:1-2

Trusting in Adonai determines our purpose and direction in life. Abram discovered Adonai as His Lord and Master when he asked, "O Lord GOD, what will You give me, since I am childless?" (Genesis 15:2). We can choose which ambitions to pursue, which master to serve, and which agendas to respond to. When Adonai is the one we follow, He is our motivation, our Master, and our mentor. To serve the living God, we must say yes to His lordship in our lives. We need to trust in the name of Adonai. Who determines our decisions, who guides our actions, and who commands our obedience? His name is Adonai.

DISCOVER ADONAI

We see God revealed as Adonai for the first time in Genesis 15:2 in the words of Abram, responding to God's promise to be his shield and his great reward: "O Lord GOD, what will you give me, since I am childless?" The Hebrew word translated "Lord" is *Adonai* and means master and owner. In the Old Testament, *Adonai* is translated "Lord" (initial capital only) in contrast to Yahweh, translated "LORD" (small capitals or all capitals). *Adonai* is used approximately 300 times in the Old Testament and is related to *kurios* ("Lord") in the New Testament. *Adonai* is almost always plural in form (pointing to the Trinity, as in *Elohim*) and possessive ("my Lord's").[1]

DRAW NEAR TO ADONAI

Knowing God as Adonai means you understand His claim on your life. Knowing Adonai as your Lord, Master, and Owner places you in the position of a servant who obeys and serves. Abram surely knew Adonai as his Master and willingly followed Him wherever He led. Lordship includes complete possession and submission; Abraham "acknowledged [God's] complete possession of and perfect right to all that he was and had."[2] As the slave experienced benefits from the master, including protection, help, direction, and affection, so you will be blessed by knowing and trusting in Adonai. Your relationship with Adonai alters the course of your life. When Daniel prayed for the sins of his nation, he acknowledged his own reverence for Adonai, acknowledging Him again and again in his prayer: "O Lord, hear! O Lord, forgive! O Lord, listen and take action!" (Daniel 9:19).

Adonai notices the service of His servants, and He is brokenhearted when His servants choose to walk away from Him or dishonor Him. When God spoke to the disobedient priests of Israel, He revealed the heart of Adonai, saying, "A son honors his father, and a servant his master. If I am a father, where is the honor due me? If I am a master, where is the respect due me?" (Malachi 1:6 NIV).

In studying the master-servant relationship in the Old Testament, a beautiful picture emerges. A Hebrew servant was required to serve his master for six years (Exodus 21:2-6). However, his master was to set him free in the seventh year without requiring any payment for freedom. But then, if the servant loved his master and did not want to go free, he could choose to continue serving his master. To seal the relationship, the master brought his servant before judges, took him to a doorpost, and pierced his ear with an awl, signifying lifelong ownership. The slave who loved his master was now his servant for life.

Trusting in Jesus as Lord

"You call Me Teacher and Lord; and you are right, for so I am" (John 13:13).

Adonai is Master and Owner of those who love their master so much so that they are servants for life. This picture of Adonai is confirmed in the lordship of Jesus Christ, who is "the radiance of God's glory and the exact representation of his being" (Hebrews 1:3 NIV). If you want to understand who God is and what He does, look at Jesus and listen to Him, for "He [Jesus] has explained Him [God]" (John 1:18).

Jesus often spoke in parables and instructional teaching about serving God. He said, "No one can serve two masters...you cannot serve God and wealth" (Matthew 6:24). "Who then is the faithful and sensible slave...blessed is that slave whom his master finds so doing when he comes" (Matthew 24:45-46). "His master said to him, 'Well done, good and faithful slave. You were faithful with a few things, I will put you in charge of many things; enter into the joy of your master'" (Matthew 25:21). "Blessed are those slaves whom the master will find on the alert when he comes" (Luke 12:37). Jesus said to His disciples, "If anyone wishes to come after Me, he must deny himself, and take up his cross and follow Me. For whoever wishes to save his life will lose it; but whoever loses his life for My sake will find it" (Matthew 16:24-25).

Because of Jesus' obedience on the cross, you have been "bought with a price" (1 Corinthians 6:20). Paul, in fact, called himself a "bond-servant of Christ Jesus" (Romans 1:1). The Greek word translated "bond-servant" is *doulos* and refers to a servant who willingly chooses to serve his master, completely belonging to his owner and having no freedom to leave.[3]

If you want to understand what it means to serve Adonai, look at the example of Jesus and how He lived His life on earth. Jesus "made himself nothing, taking the very nature of a servant, being made in human likeness. And being found in appearance as a man, he humbled himself and became obedient to death—even death on a cross" (Philippians 2:7-8 NIV). Jesus served His Father and delighted to do His will. He told His disciples, "My food is to do the will of Him who sent Me and to accomplish His work" (John 4:34). Because of Jesus' obedience to God, "he was pierced for our transgressions, he was crushed for our iniquities; the punishment that brought us peace was upon him, and by his wounds we are healed" (Isaiah 53:5 NIV). Hear the heart of the ultimate servant, your Lord, who says to His Father, "Sacrifice and offering you did not desire, but a body you prepared for me; with burnt offerings and sin offerings you were not pleased. Then I said, 'Here I am—it is written about me in the scroll—I have come to do your will, O God'" (Hebrews 10:5-7 NIV).

What does knowing Adonai tell you about yourself? You are meant to be God's servant. Adonai is looking for those servants who will say, "Here I am." He can do amazing works through those who will, like Jesus, say, "I delight to do Your will."

DECLARE ADONAI

Discovering Adonai does not simply suggest a response, but demands a decisive declaration from you. Run to Adonai and cry out, *Adonai, here I am. I delight to do Your will. Send me where You will. Use me how You will. Mold me as You will.* Then speak to your mind, your heart, and your soul, *I no longer belong to myself, but to the Lord. I have been bought with a price—the life of Jesus, my Lord. He owns all rights to my possessions, to my job, my relationships, my past, and my future. I am His and He is mine—together forever.*

Finally, what shall you declare to the world about Adonai? Paul speaks of those in the church of Corinth as letters of Christ, written with the Spirit of the living God on the tablets of their hearts, "known and read by all men" (2 Corinthians 3:2-3). Your very life, lived for Adonai, who leads and guides you, is the declaration of who He is and what He does.

DEPEND ON ADONAI

Your trust and reliance on Adonai means you will support Him, submit to Him, serve Him, and act as a good steward of all He entrusts to you.

Support of Adonai. You are loyal to your Master above all other commitments. In fact, Jesus puts it this way: "He who loves father or mother more than Me is not worthy of Me; and he who loves son or daughter more than Me is not worthy of Me. And he who does not take his cross and follow after Me is not worthy of Me" (Matthew 10:37-38). Your loyalty to Adonai includes a decision to respond to His call to follow Him above all others and say, *Yes, Lord. As for me and my house, we will follow You and live for You* (see Joshua 24:15).

Submission to Adonai. James says to "submit therefore to God" (James 4:7). This submission includes clothing yourself with humility (1 Peter 5:5). Adonai is your Master, and you are His slave and His bondservant. In Dr. Bill Bright's foreword to my book *Revive My Heart!* he mentioned a prayer and a contract he and his wife, Vonette, signed so many years ago. They prayed, *Lord, we surrender our lives irrevocably to You and to do Your will. We want to love and serve You with all of our hearts for the rest of our lives.* Dr. Bright described their experience: "We actually wrote and signed a contract committing our whole lives to Him, relinquishing all of our rights, all of our possessions, everything we would ever own, giving Him, our dear Lord and Master, everything." He continued, "That Sunday afternoon, in the words of the apostle Paul, Vonette and I became voluntary slaves of Jesus, by choice, as an act of our wills."[4] Will you do the same? Will you become a voluntary slave of Jesus Christ?

Service to Adonai. As your Master, Adonai has given you gifts and ministries. He has a desired effect in His mind for your life's service to Him (1 Corinthians 12:4-6). In fact, your whole life is dedicated to serving your Lord if you have said yes to Adonai. When you wake up in the morning, take time to sit alone with your Lord and hear what He has to say to you in His Word.

Art DeMoss, a true servant of the Lord with Campus Crusade for Christ, used to speak about the importance of his own quiet time before facing the heavy responsibilities of the day. His daughter relates that he gave the first hour of every day to the study of God's Word and prayer. Set aside a time, a place, and a plan for quiet time with Adonai in preparation for the service of the day.

Stewardship from Adonai. Jesus speaks of the wise, sensible, and faithful servant. If you would rely on Adonai, you will serve Him faithfully and regard everything you do as a stewardship entrusted to you (1 Corinthians 9:17; Colossians 1:25). And what has God entrusted? He has given you time, talents, and treasure. Hudson Taylor said, "If He is not Lord of all, He is not Lord at all."[5]

Many years ago I stood in a room with a thousand other students and said, *Lord, my name is Catherine. Here I am. Send me.* That declaration signified a commitment from me to say, *Adonai, You are my Lord, Master, and Owner. Pierce my ear to signify that I'm yours forever.* Sitting on my writing desk is a little wood plaque with the words, "Jesus Is Lord." Those words constantly remind me whose I am—His, forever.

DELIGHT IN ADONAI

Joachim Neander lived in Germany in the 1600s and studied theology at Bremen University. He loved to sing and write poetry. He lived only 30 years, but he gave us a wonderful tribute to Adonai: "Praise to the Lord, the Almighty," perfect words for those who would delight in Adonai.

> Praise to the Lord, the Almighty, the King of creation!
> O my soul, praise Him, for He is thy health and salvation!
> All ye who hear, now to His temple draw near;
> Praise Him in glad adoration.
>
> Praise to the Lord, who over all things so wondrously reigneth,
> Shelters thee under His wings, yea, so gently sustaineth!
> Hast thou not seen how thy desires ever have been
> Granted in what He ordaineth?
>
> Praise to the Lord, who doth prosper thy work and defend thee;
> Surely His goodness and mercy here daily attend thee.
> Ponder anew what the Almighty can do,
> If with His love He befriend thee.
>
> Praise to the Lord, O let all that is in me adore Him!
> All that hath life and breath, come now with praises before Him.
> Let the Amen sound from His people again,
> Gladly for aye we adore Him.

DATE:

KEY VERSE: "O Lord God, what will You give me, since I am childless?" (Genesis 15:2).

FOR FURTHER THOUGHT: Imagine this is the seventh year for you, a servant. Do you love Adonai, your Master, such that you will say, *Pierce my ear, Lord. I love You and will serve You forever.* Write a prayer of commitment to Adonai, expressing all that is on your heart.

MY RESPONSE:

Day Sixteen

TRUSTING IN EL SHADDAI—HE IS ENOUGH FOR YOU

I am God Almighty. Walk before Me and be blameless.

GENESIS 17:1

Trusting in El Shaddai brings you to the place of abundance, where you experience overflowing satisfaction. El Shaddai is the all-sufficient one who appeared to Abram and said, "I am God Almighty. Walk before Me and be blameless" (Genesis 17:1). The discovery of God as El Shaddai marked a new day for Abram. He realized God was more than he had known Him to be and that God was able to accomplish all He had promised. Knowing God as El Shaddai brought Abram into a more intimate relationship with God and gave him a bold and courageous faith. He believed God and became a friend of God (James 2:23). Do you long to be a friend of God? Are you bold and courageous in your relationship with God? Run to El Shaddai.

DISCOVER EL SHADDAI

When God revealed Himself to Abram as God Almighty, He was also proclaiming a new name for Himself, *El Shaddai. El Shaddai* means "God, the powerful one" or "God, the mighty one."[1] As a divine name, *Shaddai* or *El Shaddai* is used 48 times in the Old Testament, 31 occurring in the book of Job. *Shaddai* comes from the Hebrew root *shad,* meaning "breast," and gives us a precious metaphor, presenting God as "the one who nourishes, supplies, and satisfies."[2] In *El Shaddai,* we learn that God possesses all power, unlimited supply, and infinite blessing. He is the all-sufficient one, the omnipotent God, who has never-ending bounty for His people. G. Campbell Morgan calls El Shaddai the "God all-bountiful" or "God all-sufficient," derived from the literal meaning of "the mighty one of resource or sufficiency."[3]

DRAW NEAR TO EL SHADDAI

How can you get close to El Shaddai and experience Him in your own life? The best way is to understand His nature and why He would want you to know Him as El Shaddai. Remember, He gives His names so you might enter into a deeper, more intimate relationship with Him. God's revelation to Abraham resulted in friendship with God. The same may be true for you—you can experience friendship with God by drawing near to El Shaddai.

El Shaddai was the name of God known especially to the patriarchs (Abraham, Isaac, and Jacob). For example, when God revealed Himself as El Shaddai to Abram, He confirmed His covenant with Abram, who was 99 years of age and seemingly beyond hope of fathering a child. El Shaddai changed his name to Abraham, meaning "father of a multitude," affirming His power to accomplish His promise. Isaac blessed his son Jacob in the name of El Shaddai (Genesis 28:3), and Jacob received a confirmation of the covenant from El Shaddai at Bethel (Genesis 35:9-13).

When you think of El Shaddai, think of the word *power*—in this case, the power of an almighty, all-powerful God. Our finite minds are unable to comprehend God's unlimited power or even His ability to command the laws of nature He created. One night, while away on a writing trip for this book, I was wakened by a loud noise, the rattling of bottles in the bathroom, and then the shaking of my door. I panicked. Was someone in my room? Then my room began swaying back and forth for many interminable seconds. As suddenly as the shaking had begun, it stopped. Later, I discovered my hotel room was a mere four miles from the epicenter of an earthquake.

Earthquakes are nothing new to anyone who lives in Southern California. However, if you've ever been at the epicenter of one of these events as I was, or as my brother was in the 5.9 Whittier earthquake in 1987, you can begin to catch a glimpse of the awesome nature of God's great power. His power is known as His *omnipotence.*

Stephen Charnock, author of one of the great books on the character of God, wrote, "The power of God is that ability and strength whereby He can bring to pass whatsoever He pleases, whatsoever His infinite wisdom can direct, and whatsoever the infinite purity of His will can resolve."[4] Contemplating the power of God brings you to the great realization of Paul that "God is able" (Romans 16:25; 2 Corinthians 9:8; Ephesians 3:20-21; see also Jude 1:24).

God is able to match any need you have with His unlimited power. The Lord rhetorically asked Abraham, "Is anything too difficult for the LORD?" (Genesis 18:14) when He observed Sarah laughing at the possibility of bearing a child at such an advanced age. When Jeremiah questioned the Lord, he was met with the same question from God: "Is anything too difficult for Me?" (Jeremiah 32:27). Our conclusion must match Jeremiah's: "Ah Lord GOD! Behold, You have made the heavens and the earth by Your great power and by Your outstretched arm! Nothing is too difficult for You" (Jeremiah 32:17).

The name *El Shaddai* reminds us of God's unlimited supply of comfort, power, grace, and more—in fact, a sufficient supply of anything you need. In her book *The God of All Comfort,* Hannah Whitall Smith speaks of her own discovery that God is enough. Hannah visited a godly woman and poured out her heart, revealing great pain and sorrow over her adversities.

The woman replied, "Yes, all you may say may be very true, but then, in spite of it all, there is God."

Hannah waited for something more and became frustrated because her teacher and friend acted as though she had said all that was necessary. Hannah said, "But surely you did not understand how very serious and perplexing my difficulties are."

Her friend responded, "Oh, yes I did, but then, as I tell you, there is God." Hannah shares her amazing discovery:

> I began dimly to wonder whether after all God might not be enough, even for my need, overwhelming and peculiar as I felt it to be. From wondering I came gradually to believing, that, being my Creator and Redeemer, He must be enough; and at last a conviction burst upon me that He really was enough, and my eyes were opened to the fact of the absolute and utter all-sufficiency of God.[5]

What does knowing El Shaddai tell you about yourself? God is sufficient, and you are not. Therefore, you need Him. God abundantly supplies your every need—grace, goodness, mercy, kindness, strength, comfort—whatever your need may be. He is enough.

Trusting in Jesus as All-Sufficient

"He has said to me, 'My grace is sufficient for you, for power is perfected in weakness'" (2 Corinthians 12:9).

Paul's thorn in the flesh prompted him to implore the Lord for removal of the torment. But Jesus proclaimed His all-sufficiency to Paul. He was enough for Paul's greatest weakness. In fact, the greater the obstacle, the more Paul would experience the power of Christ. And because Jesus is the exact representation of God (Hebrews 1:3), all believers can experience the power of El Shaddai in their lives as Jesus now lives in them (Galatians 2:20) through the indwelling Holy Spirit (Romans 8:9-10).

DECLARE EL SHADDAI

When you doubt your own ability to fulfill your calling, whether it is great ministry, a great responsibility, or a great suffering, run to El Shaddai, and say, *El Shaddai, You are able. You are able to make all grace abound to me, so that having all sufficiency in everything, I may have an abundance for every good deed* (2 Corinthians 9:8). Say to your own mind, heart, and soul in both the difficult and even in the easy circumstances of life, *Nothing is too difficult for God. El Shaddai is my sufficiency!* Read these words of Isaac Watts as he declares El Shaddai to the world:

> I sing the mighty power of God that made the mountains rise,
> That spread the flowing seas abroad and built the lofty skies.
> I sing the wisdom that ordained the sun to rule the day;
> The moon shines full at His command, and all the stars obey.

DEPEND ON EL SHADDAI

Perhaps no other name inspires a greater faith and trust than *El Shaddai*. Knowing El Shaddai will light the fire of devotion in your heart. Drawing near to El Shaddai will make you a radical disciple in your generation. Loving El Shaddai will set you apart from many in your culture as you dare to do mighty things in His power and strength. You will be like Billy Graham, who loved God so much he dared to preach to stadiums of thousands. You will be like George Mueller, a nineteenth-century evangelist and philanthropist, who believed God for millions of dollars to build orphanages in England. You will be like King David, who, as a young boy, dared to slay a giant. No obstacles will defeat you, nothing will be impossible for you, because you know El Shaddai, the one who is greater than any difficulty.

When El Shaddai calls you to Himself, He will inspire you to great tasks and sometimes even great suffering and sorrows. Adoniram Judson, credited as the first American missionary to go overseas, was clear about his call to go to Burma. His task was a great one and included translating the first Burmese Bible, enabling those in Burma to read and study God's Word, changing their lives forever. But Judson's hardships were many, including the loss of children and two wives as well as devastating illnesses. He found God to be equal to the magnitude of the task, loss, or illness. At the end of his life, within days of his death, he wrote this:

> Lying here on my bed, when I could not talk, I have had such views of the loving condescension of Christ and the glories of heaven as I believe are seldom granted to mortal man...I am

not tired of my work, neither am I tired of the world. Yet when Christ calls me home, I shall go with the gladness of a boy bounding away from his school. Perhaps I feel something like the young bride, when she contemplates resigning the pleasant associations of her childhood for a yet dearer home—though only a very little like her, for there is no doubt resting on my future…I feel so strong in Christ.[6]

God's sufficiency is always more than a match for our urgency.

El Shaddai will inspire you to great prayer. God expects us to ask Him for great things (Jeremiah 33:3) and wants us to pray instead of worry (Philippians 4:6-7). So many talk about the need for revival. But how many talk with God about the need for revival? Evan Roberts, a Welsh coal miner, began praying for revival in Wales at the age of 13. When he was 26, he was profoundly moved by God to travel throughout Wales, preaching the gospel. Roberts was the catalyst for the great Welsh Revival of 1904–1905. In 1906, God raised up another Welsh coal miner, Rees Howells, to pray for others who had been spiritually changed as a result of the Welsh Revival. His prayer ministry led to the founding of a Bible College in Wales, where thousands learned the importance of intercessory prayer.

El Shaddai will inspire you to a great faith like Abraham's. Faith pleases God (Hebrews 11:6) and is the victory that overcomes the world (1 John 5:4). V. Raymond Edman, former president of Wheaton College, spoke of the discipline of a daring faith: "To dare, when God is for us and is leading us, is to defy the human impossibilities until the outcome is complete triumph. Daring can mean the difference between defeat by default and the delight of duty well done."[7] His often-quoted motto was, "Not somehow, but triumphantly." When you realize that nothing is too difficult for God, you will believe Him for mighty things, even seemingly impossible things. You will walk by faith with your eyes fixed on El Shaddai and not on the giant obstacles in your life.

El Shaddai will inspire you to be a person of great endurance. Edman calls endurance the discipline of durability and says we must "endure 'as seeing him who is invisible' when all manner of cruelty is concocted against you: contempt, complaint, criticism, condemnation, or conspiracy." He says, "The Invisible Christ will not fail you. Walk in His Presence; and find His power, provision and protection from all evil. Having done all, stand!"[8] When you trust in El Shaddai, you will learn never to give up as you watch God match your need with His sufficiency regardless of the depth of the challenge.

DELIGHT IN EL SHADDAI

Abram was 99 years old when God appeared to him and spoke with him. As we contemplate this momentous event in the life of Abram, we have before us solid proof that our God is not a distant God, but one who is personal and breaks in on our lives, initiating a personal, intimate, vibrant relationship. Genesis 17:1 says the Lord appeared to Abram and spoke to him. God makes his Presence known and also speaks—two vital actions for any relationship. He has made His presence known to us through His creation (Psalm 19:1), through Jesus (John 1:14), and, when we receive Christ as our Savior and Lord, through the Holy Spirit (Romans 8:11). God speaks with us now by the Holy Spirit through His Word, the Bible (Hebrews 4:12).

When God appeared to Abram and spoke, Abram fell facedown before God (Genesis 17:3). Can you do any less when you experience God's presence and hear Him speak? Delighting in El Shaddai today means worshipping with your entire life, bowing your heart in sheer reverence for your Almighty God, the powerful one, who has unlimited supply and is able to do "immeasurably more than all we ask or imagine, according to his power that is at work within us" (Ephesians 3:20 NIV). "To him be glory in the church and in Christ Jesus throughout all generations, for ever and ever! Amen" (Ephesians 3:21 NIV).

My Response

DATE:

KEY VERSE: "I am God Almighty. Walk before Me and be blameless" (Genesis 17:1).

FOR FURTHER THOUGHT: What is the most significant truth you have learned about El Shaddai? Why do you need El Shaddai? How will knowing El Shaddai change how you live your life?

MY RESPONSE:

TRUSTING IN YAHWEH JIREH—HE IS YOUR PROVIDER

Abraham called the name of that place The LORD Will Provide.

GENESIS 22:14

Trusting in Yahweh Jireh carries you to the other side of tests of faith. Yahweh Jireh ("the LORD will provide") gives you hope blended with faith, and the result is TRUST, which we've seen is Total Reliance Under Stress and Trial. Abraham discovered Yahweh Jireh in the greatest test of his life, greater even than leaving his home for an unknown land, greater even than a desolate nomadic life, and greater even than believing God for a child when he and his wife were past the age of childbearing. God asked Abraham to sacrifice his only son, Isaac. But Abraham soon discovered that God is greater than any sacrifice, even the sacrifice of his beloved son. When Abraham discovered this name of God, he called the place of his testing, "The LORD Will Provide" (Genesis 22:14). Where do you run when your faith is tested to the brink of failure, to the point of doubting what God has promised? Dear friend, run to Yahweh Jireh and discover that what He has said, He will do—the Lord will provide.

DISCOVER YAHWEH JIREH

The Hebrew words translated "The LORD Will Provide" are *Yahweh (YHWH) yir'eh*, and are read as the English transliteration, *Yahweh Jireh*. Contained in the meaning of this name is a wonderful combination of two attributes of God: the Lord will see, and the Lord will provide. Lockyer explains that "because of His omniscience (all-knowing) and perfection of character, He is able to provide for, or supply, the need whatever it may be."[1] *Yahweh Jireh* might be amplified and understood as "the Lord will see to it."[2]

DRAW NEAR TO YAHWEH JIREH

Abraham was a friend of God. And yet in Genesis 22:1 we see that God tested Abraham. A test from God proves what is true, real, genuine, and authentic, and it results in spiritual growth and blessing. God asked the impossible of Abraham. He asked Abraham to take his son ("your only son, whom you love, Isaac"—Genesis 22:2) and sacrifice him as a burnt offering on a mountain that He would show Abraham.

What was God's intent? I believe God revealed His purpose following the event, only after Abraham obediently tied Isaac on the altar and lifted the knife to kill him. God stopped Abraham and then told him, "Now I know you fear God, because you have not withheld from me your son, your only son" (Genesis 22:12 NIV). This test from God was a proof of Abraham's heart—did he fear God? The Hebrew word translated "fear" is *yare* and means awe or reverence. Did Abraham surrender his son, Isaac, easily? I believe the name *Yahweh Jireh* reveals the depth of Abraham's pain, emotion, and adversity in the surrender of Isaac to the Lord.

After God prevented Abraham from sacrificing Isaac, He provided a ram for the burnt offering. At the zenith of his test of faith, Abraham knew and trusted Yahweh Jireh. He knew beyond any doubt that Yahweh Jireh saw everything on the top of that mountain—Abraham, Isaac, the verbal exchanges between father and son, and Abraham's unshakeable trust in God's provision of the lamb for the offering (Genesis 22:8).

We glean some insight into Abraham's thoughts on the mountain that day from Hebrews 11:19 (TNIV): "Abraham reasoned that God could even raise the dead, and so in a manner of speaking he did receive Isaac back from death." God saw the deepest need that day, a sacrifice to take Isaac's place, and He provided that sacrifice Himself. And Abraham passed the test of faith. Abraham learned God's name *Yahweh Jireh* and received the blessings of obedience from the Lord (Genesis 22:15-18).

When God tries a heart, He teaches the heart. He moves people to a new place in their relationship with Him through a process of surrender and seasons of growth. Trials are tests of faith and produce endurance, that great quality that is absolutely necessary to make it to the finish line (James 1:3). God tested the people of Israel in the wilderness, humbling them for the benefit of their spiritual growth. God wanted to show them what was in their own hearts, to encourage their obedience to His commandments, and to help them understand that real life comes from faith in what He says—"everything that proceeds out of the mouth of the LORD" (Deuteronomy 8:2-3). During those arduous 40 years in the wilderness, the Lord, Yahweh Jireh, provided for the deep needs of His people by feeding, clothing, leading, and guiding them. And He will do the same for you in the depth of your needs.

Peter's first letter in the New Testament includes many references to suffering. He speaks of trials as "proof of your faith" (1 Peter 1:7). When your faith is tested by fire and shown to be genuine, the final result will be praise and glory in the future when you see Christ. There is so much at stake in trials, or "fiery ordeals," as Peter calls them (1 Peter 4:12), when your faith is tested. Your spiritual growth, the strengthening of your faith, and other blessings are all results of a test of faith. You can rest in your trial when you know Yahweh Jireh, the Lord who provides.

What does knowing Yahweh Jireh tell you about yourself? You have needs that can be met only by your Lord. And how do you respond when God asks the seemingly impossible of you? The impossible becomes possible when you know and trust in Yahweh Jireh.

Trusting in Jesus as Provider

"God will supply all your needs according to His riches in glory in Christ Jesus" (Philippians 4:19).

When you are in the heat of any trial, Yahweh Jireh sees you and provides for you. Philippians 4:19 is your great promise to find, embrace, trust, and live out in your own life. Yahweh Jireh has always provided for His people in the heat of their trials—a sacrifice in place of Isaac, manna for His people in the desert, His presence for Daniel in the lion's den, and the resurrection of Jesus. The cross is His ultimate provision as Jesus paid the price for our sin. And you can know that in your trial, the great test of your faith, Yahweh Jireh will see your deepest need and provide for you through Jesus Christ.

DECLARE YAHWEH JIREH

When you question how you are going to make it, when you find yourself doubting the truth of God's Word, or when you wonder how God can possibly help you in your trial, you must run to Yahweh Jireh, asking Him to provide for you. *Yahweh Jireh, you know my heart, fears, doubts, and questions. I am coming to You, the one who provided for Abraham, Moses, David, Daniel, and so many others. I ask You to provide all I need in this testing of my faith. May I stand strong in the promises of Your Word, and may You get all the glory and honor.* Then, speak to your mind, heart, and soul, "The LORD will provide for all my needs according to His riches in glory in Christ Jesus" (Philippians 4:19).

And then, what shall you declare to the world about Yahweh Jireh? Stand strong in the Lord, dear friend, for your steadfast spirit and your faith in Christ through the trial is speaking volumes to the world. And you can rest in the promise that your troubles are resulting in perseverance, proven character, and hope (Romans 5:3-5).

DEPEND ON YAHWEH JIREH

All of us have Isaacs that must be placed on the altar—the death of a dream or the loss of a child, our health, a job, or financial security. These surrenders often test our faith. What constitutes a test of our faith? In a test, what you know to be true in the Bible is challenged by how you feel, what you think, or what you see happening in your life circumstances. Most importantly, recognize the nature of the event—it is a test of faith. That recognition alone provides a sense of relief.

Calculate into your circumstance what you know to be true. Ask yourself, *What does God say in His Word?* Then ask, *What do I need to lay aside in order to grasp the promise of God?* You may have to let go of certain beliefs or thoughts or perspectives that are contrary to the Word of God. You may have to let go of desperate or even delightful dreams of what you think your life should look like in order to grasp the promise of God.

Dwight Hervey Small, in his book *No Rival Love,* speaks to the sunny side of surrender:

> When we give up ourselves in heart, mind, and will to God, He becomes ours to possess and enjoy! When we cease to be our own, we become His. When we lose ourselves in Him, we find ourselves. Being content to relinquish ourselves, we possess ourselves more truly than ever. But God usually hides the solution to faith's riddle until the very last moment of a trial, so that our faith may develop fully. God, who undertakes a perfect work in us, is never too late in His intervention for us, never too early. His ways are perfect—in us and for us.[3]

Some of the greatest tests of our faith rapidly exhaust every possible resource, forcing us to look upon God's provision as our only hope. Some, at the point of hopelessness, have described a feeling of being trapped, as though they had no way out. Tozer says, "Let me tell you with assurance that the happy Christian is the one who has been caught—captured by the Lord. He or she no longer wants to escape or go back. The happy Christian has met the Lord personally and found Him an all sufficient Savior and Lord. He or she has burned all the bridges in every direction."[4]

Tests of faith measure the depth of your commitment to your Lord. Such was the case for Abraham in the surrender of Isaac. Some have only a shallow commitment, unable to bear the heat of any trial whatsoever. When the Israelites were tested in the wilderness, even with constant provision from the Lord, they constantly complained with every new difficulty. We know that God was not pleased that they were "laid low in the wilderness" (1 Corinthians 10:5). Tozer speaks of shallow commitment:

> Some of God's children are dabbling with surrender and victory. They have never reached that place of spiritual commitment which is final and complete and satisfying. They still retain their escape routes...they have never willingly given up their doors of retreat. They can get out any time they want to. They can appear to be walking with the Lord as long as things are normal. But when the tight spot comes, the time of crisis, they opt out.[5]

Abraham's commitment was strong for the Lord—he had no earthly retreat, recourse, or resource. More importantly, he desired none.

When you have cast yourself upon God, do you have any hope in your time of loss or difficulty, whatever it may be? Yes, because the Lord promises He will provide for you (Philippians 4:19). Trusting in God's promises when you cannot imagine how He will carry out His plan demonstrates to Him your great faith. Faith pleases God, and when He knows He can have His way with you, He provides in the most amazing and miraculous ways. God is not blind to our desperate needs, nor does He provide in hit-or-miss fashion. He sees exactly, with complete understanding, and provides specifically for your exact need.

Keep in mind that your interpretation of your need may be quite different from God's interpretation. We know that God's thoughts are not our thoughts, nor are His ways our ways. God explains this truth further in Isaiah 55:10 by telling us, "For as the heavens are higher than the earth, so are My ways higher than your ways and My thoughts than your thoughts."

Mary, Martha, and Lazarus were three of Jesus' best friends. After long days of ministry, Jesus would often travel to Bethany to spend time with them. One day Jesus received a message from Mary and Martha that Lazarus was deathly sick. Jesus loved Lazarus and could have immediately departed for Bethany to heal him. But instead, "He then stayed two days longer in the place where He was" (John 11:6). He then told His disciples that Lazarus was asleep, but He was going to wake him up.

The disciples thought He meant a natural sleep and told Jesus that Lazarus would get better since he was able to sleep. Jesus then spoke plainly with His disciples: "Lazarus is dead, and for your sake I am glad I was not there, so that you may believe" (John 11:14-15 NIV). Jesus wanted their faith to grow and was about to perform a greater miracle than anyone could have thought possible. To perform that miracle meant not healing Lazarus while he was sick, but instead raising Lazarus from the dead.

By the time Jesus arrived in Bethany, Lazarus had already been dead four days. Mary and Martha were devastated. Martha ran to Jesus and told Him that if He had been there, Lazarus would not have died. Jesus challenged Martha's faith and told her Lazarus would rise again. Jesus told her that He was the resurrection and the life. What more could she want? He then asked her, "Do you believe this?" Mary, her sister, fell at the feet of Jesus, weeping, and told Him that His presence would have prevented Lazarus from dying.

When Jesus arrives at the tomb, we are given a glimpse into the heart of God. In John 11:35, we see that "Jesus wept." These two words show us that the Lord feels deep emotion and shares our pain in the midst of our suffering. Don't ever forget that. Life is not just an academic university filled with tests and learning. Life involves walking with Jesus in an intimate relationship, sharing His heart and letting Him share your heart. He provides hope, comfort, and encouragement when you are feeling pain. He will deliver you out of your difficulty, or through your difficulty, taking you to the other side of the testing of your faith.

In the case of His three friends at Bethany, Jesus, deeply moved, went to the tomb and told those who were there to take the stone away from the door of the cave. He said, "Did I not tell you that if you believe, you will see the glory of God?" (John 11:40 TNIV). After the stone was removed, Jesus prayed to His Father, thanked Him, and expressed His desire that those who were in attendance would believe that He had been sent from God. Then Jesus called out in a loud voice, "Lazarus, come out!" Lazarus indeed walked out of the cave with his hands and feet still wrapped in linen and the grave cloth still on his face.

Can you imagine the emotion of this miraculous scene? Jesus gives the command, and a dead man comes to life and walks out of a tomb. The text tells us that many who saw that miracle put their faith in Jesus (John 11:45). You see, Jesus did not do what everyone wanted by coming to Bethany early in order to heal Lazarus. Through perfect timing, God's timing, He performed a miracle of raising Lazarus from the dead, resulting in a new faith and a new belief for many and increasing the faith of those around Him who were being trained for His high purposes. Always know that God's ways, though different from our own, are always perfect and result in His greatest good and highest glory.

DELIGHT IN YAHWEH JIREH

How do you delight in the Lord when Yahweh Jireh provides for you? When Jesus healed ten lepers, one of them stepped out of the crowd in his praise for the Lord. He turned back, glorified God, fell on his face before the Lord Jesus, and said thank You. Take time, when God provides for you, to say thank You to Him.

DATE:

KEY VERSE: "Abraham called the name of that place The LORD Will Provide" (Genesis 22:14).

FOR FURTHER THOUGHT: How is your faith being tested? Is there an Isaac in your life that you need to lay down to be wholeheartedly surrendered to the Lord? What meant the most to you in the example of the raising of Lazarus? How do you need Yahweh Jireh today, the one who sees the heart of your need and provides for you?

MY RESPONSE:

QUIET TIME WEEK THREE: TRUSTING GOD AS ABRAHAM DID

And the Scripture was fulfilled which says, "And Abraham believed God, and it was reckoned to him as righteousness" and he was called the friend of God.

JAMES 2:23

PREPARE YOUR HEART

One of the heroes in the Bible who lived a life of great faith and devotion is Abraham. How can we be like Abraham, who trusted in El Elyon to control all the affairs of his life, who looked to El Shaddai for power and sufficiency in all he was required to do, and who served Adonai as his Lord, Master, and Owner? Today we will take some time with Abraham and look more deeply at his relationship with the Lord. Ask the Lord to speak to your heart as you sit with Him in your quiet time today.

READ AND STUDY GOD'S WORD

1. One of the great standout heroes in Genesis is, without a doubt, Abraham. How can one not admire a person who would be willing to give up everything to go out to an unknown country simply because God asked him to do it? Read the following passages of Scripture about Abraham

and record your most significant insights about his relationship with the Lord.

Genesis 12:1-4

Genesis 12:7-8

Genesis 15:1-6

Genesis 17:1-8

Genesis 21:1-3

2. Abraham is such a hero of the faith that he is spoken of often in the New Testament. Look at the following verses and record what you learn about Abraham:

Romans 4:18-23

Hebrews 11:8-10

Hebrews 11:13-19

James 2:23

3. What is the most important truth you have learned from the life of Abraham that you can apply to your own life?

ADORE GOD IN PRAYER

Did you notice Abraham's habit of building an altar to remember God and worship Him? Take some time now to draw near, talk with Him, and worship.

YIELD YOURSELF TO GOD

> The keynote of Abram's life was *separation,* step by step, until country, kindred, Lot, worldly alliances, and fleshly expedients were one by one cast aside and he stood alone with God! Though he knew not whither he went, the father of the faithful obeyed and crossed the wide and perilous deserts. It was this absolute and unquestioning obedience that endeared him to God. Let us ever obey and step out, though it seems as though there were naught but seething mist. We shall find it solid under the tread of faith...The tent life is natural to the man whose portion is God; and where he pitches his tent, he will rear his altar.[1]
>
> F.B. MEYER

ENJOY HIS PRESENCE

Friend, where have you pitched your tent today? With the Lord or with the world? Will you stand with your Elohim, El Elyon, Yahweh Jireh, El Shaddai, and Adonai, pitch your tent on His holy ground, build an altar there, and worship Him? Then you, my friend, like Abraham, may be called a friend of God. Close your time today by writing a prayer to your Lord, expressing all that is on your heart.

REST IN HIS LOVE

"But as it is, they desire a better country, that is, a heavenly one. Therefore God is not ashamed to be called their God; for He has prepared a city for them" (Hebrews 11:16).

Notes—Week Three

Week Four

DISCOVERING GOD'S PERSON AND PRESENCE

Days 19–24

Day Nineteen

TRUSTING IN EL ROI—HE SEES YOU

*You are the God who sees me...I have
now seen the One who sees me. That is
why the well was called Beer Lahai Roi.*

GENESIS 16:13-14 NIV

Trusting in El Roi brings you comfort when you feel alone. Because your God is El Roi, "the one who sees you," you can know you are always under His watchful care. God revealed Himself as El Roi to an Egyptian maidservant who was harshly treated and fled to the desert. Hagar, an Egyptian woman, was the handmaid to Sarah, given by Sarah to Abraham as a concubine to produce an heir. Not once, but twice, Hagar fled a hostile situation and Sarah's wrath. And not once, but twice, the angel of the Lord saw Hagar's distress and comforted her. After God met her in the wilderness, Hagar said, " 'You are the God who sees me...I have now seen the One who sees me.' That is why the well was called Beer Lahai Roi" (Genesis 16:13-14 NIV). Who is this God who would meet an outcast servant in the desert? Who is the God who will meet you in your wilderness experience? Who is this God who cares about the most minute details of your suffering? His name is *El Roi*.

DISCOVER EL ROI

God's name *El Roi* is curiously found only in the desperate situation of Hagar in Genesis 16:13-14 and nowhere else in Scripture. These Hebrew words imply that your God sees you regardless of where you are, how you feel, or what circumstances you face. *Ra'ah* is a common Hebrew verb for literal, physical sight (as in Genesis 27:1). But *ro'i* has extended and metaphorical meanings too. In Hagar's case, the Lord shows He cares for her. As Gordon Wenham points out in the *Word Biblical Commentary,* "When God sees it, he cares (cf. Genesis 29:32; Exodus 3:7)."[1] "The LORD said, 'I have surely seen the affliction of My people...for I am aware of their sufferings'" (Exodus 3:7). The God who comforted Hagar in the desert is the very same one who delivered Israel from Egypt. When God sees, He cares, He delivers, and He acts on your behalf.

DRAW NEAR TO EL ROI

Contemplating El Roi takes you into the presence of God, a most precious and awesome experience. Why? Your realization that God sees you regardless of where you are emphasizes God's nearness in your life. Resisting God's command to preach to Nineveh, Jonah "fled from the presence of the LORD," or so he thought. But neither wind, nor rain, nor the belly of the fish could separate him from God's sight. Indeed, "Jonah prayed to the LORD his God from the stomach of the fish" (Jonah 2:1). You can run from people, situations, and responsibilities; you may even try to run from God, but you can never hide from El Roi.

Even though the name *El Roi* is limited to one place in Scripture, we find many references to the sight of God throughout the Bible. We know El Roi sees us in our most desperate hour because He saw Hagar and found her alone in the wilderness by a spring of water. Regardless of how desperate or abandoned you feel, El Roi is at hand, He sees you, and He will find you. El Roi saw you when you were in your mother's womb (Psalm 139:16).

Nothing is hidden from God—He sees everything (Hebrews 4:13). The psalmist tells us that "the LORD looks from heaven; He sees all the sons of men; from His dwelling place He looks out on all the inhabitants of the earth" (Psalm 33:13-14). When El Roi sees you, He will act on your behalf; He will not abandon you. We learn that "the eye of the LORD is on those who fear Him, on those who hope for His lovingkindness, to deliver their soul from death and to keep them alive in famine" (Psalm 33:18-19). Indeed, His eyes are toward the righteous, and His ears are open to their cry (Psalm 34:15).

God does not see as man sees—superficially, incompletely, and impassively. When God sent Samuel to anoint the next king after Saul, He told Samuel, "Do not look at his appearance or at the height of his stature…for God sees not as man sees, for man looks at the outward appearance, but the LORD looks at the heart" (1 Samuel 16:7). God is looking for committed hearts because He wants to "strongly support those whose heart is completely His" (2 Chronicles 16:9).

When you think about El Roi, you cannot help but think about the very presence of God. He is with you. You are not alone. And God never meant for you to be alone—He is your great Companion in life. What Moses told the people of Israel is also true for you: "The LORD your God is the one who goes with you. He will not fail you or forsake you" (Deuteronomy 31:6). Jesus promised us, "Lo, I am with you always" (Matthew 28:20). Because He is with you, you never need to fear or worry.

Knowing He is El Roi reminds you of the attention you receive from Him. Perhaps you feel as though no one sees and no one cares. El Roi notices everything about you. Jesus said that God knows when a sparrow falls to the ground and that you are of more value than many sparrows (Matthew 10:29; Luke 12:6-7). Dr. Harry A. Ironside explains poignantly, "God attends the funeral of every sparrow." In fact, God has numbered each hair on your head. If He cares to the extent of numbering the hairs on your head, you can know He sees and cares for you. He will never forget you because, according to Isaiah, He has inscribed (engraved) you on the palm of His hands (Isaiah 49:16).

When we meditate on El Roi, the one who sees us, we are venturing into the incomprehensible mystery of the omniscience of God, His infinite knowledge and wisdom. Nothing is a mystery to God. Nothing is a problem to God. No puzzles can cloud God's mind. Paul contemplated God's omniscience:

> Oh, the depth of the riches of the wisdom and knowledge of God! How unsearchable his judgments and his paths beyond tracing out! Who has known the mind of the Lord? Or who has been his counselor? Who has ever given to God, that God should repay him? For from him and through him and to him are all things. To him be the glory forever! Amen (Romans 11:33-36 NIV).

Trusting in Jesus Who Sees You

"Nathanael said to Him, 'How do You know me?' Jesus answered and said to him, 'Before Philip called you, when you were under the fig tree, I saw you'" (John 1:48).

Jesus said "I saw you" to Nathanael with the same implications that Hagar articulated when she responded to El Roi, "You are the God who sees me." Both instances demonstrate the omniscience of God. The Greek word translated "saw" in John 1:48 is *eido* and implies sight with perception, analogous to the extended metaphorical usage of *ro'i* in Hagar's rescue in the Old Testament. Jesus saw Nathanael's heart, that it harbored no deceit (John 1:47). John Henry Jowett says, "It is not only that Nathanael was noticed; it means he was understood. Our Lord's sight is insight...His perceptions were compassions...The Master not only feels, He works; He not only sympathizes, He serves. When He saw Nathaneael under the fig-tree, His understanding, His sympathy, His power, all combined in a ministry of benevolent and beneficent love." As Jesus saw and knew Nathanael, so He sees and knows you.

What does knowing El Roi tell you about yourself? You are not alone. You are also accountable. God sees everything; you are accountable in everything. You have one who is always looking out for you, who can help you and deliver you.

DECLARE EL ROI

When you feel alone and unnoticed, run to your El Roi and say, *El Roi, You are the one who sees me.* Then speak to your mind, heart, and soul and say, *The Lord will not forget me. He has engraved me on the palms of His hands. I am continually before Him.* What do you say to an impersonal world living as though God does not exist? You say, "The LORD looks from heaven; He sees all the sons of men; from His dwelling place He looks out on all the inhabitants of the earth" (Psalm 33:13-14).

DEPEND ON EL ROI

Civilla Martin and her husband were sojourning in Elmira, New York, in the spring of 1905. They became friends with a joyous couple by the name of Mr. and Mrs. Doolittle, true saints of the Lord. Mrs. Doolittle had been bed-ridden for 20 years, and her husband was also crippled, in a wheelchair. One day, while visiting the Doolittles, Civilla asked Mrs. Doolittle the secret of her hopefulness. Mrs. Doolittle's reply was simply, "His eye is on the sparrow, and I know He watches me." Civilla Martin penned the poem and mailed it to Charles Gabriel, who supplied the music. No one sees or cares like El Roi.

I asked one of my Bible study classes what knowing El Roi meant to them. A young man in the front row raised his hand, immediately convicted. He had seen some lumber abandoned in a nearby yard and had been thinking about just taking it for some time. Then came the classes on the names of God, and he learned that God was El Roi, the one who sees him. That changed everything. Knowing God was El Roi helped him see that everything he does is known and seen by God Himself. He said he could not take that lumber now, regardless of how much he wanted it. We all laughed together, realizing that knowing God as El Roi changes every aspect of our lives because God is the one who sees us. Just think—you can depend on one in your life who is always present and always sees. His name is El Roi.

DELIGHT IN EL ROI

Delighting in El Roi means you praise Him for His presence, His person, His protection, and His perception. Pray that as His eyes are moving "to and fro throughout the earth," your heart will be the one that is "wholly His" and that He will "strongly support" you (2 Chronicles 16:9). Always remember that as His eye is on the sparrow, so His eye is on you.

> Of all God's marvels transcendent,
> This wonder of wonders I see,
> That the God of such infinite greatness
> Should care for the sparrows—and me.[2]

My Response

DATE:

KEY VERSE: "'You are the God who sees me...I have now seen the One who sees me.' That is why the well was called Beer Lahai Roi" (Genesis 16:13-14 NIV).

FOR FURTHER THOUGHT: How does knowing El Roi encourage you, and how do you need Him today?

MY RESPONSE:

TRUSTING IN YAHWEH—HE IS EVERYTHING YOU NEED

God said to Moses, "I am who I am.
This is what you are to say to the
Israelites: I AM has sent me to you."

EXODUS 3:14 NIV

Trusting in God as Yahweh leads you to the most sacred, holy place in your relationship with Him, for *Yahweh* is the most personal, intimate name of God. Consider Moses, formerly a prince in Pharaoh's court, now a mere shepherd in the wilderness. Not until the second 40 years of his life would Moses stand on holy ground, face-to-face with Yahweh.

The first appearance of God to Moses came as a blazing fire from the midst of a bush that was not consumed. Moses "turned aside" to look at the "marvelous sight" but instead faced the radiant light of God's glory. And then he heard the command, "Remove your sandals from your feet, for the place on which you are standing is holy ground" (Exodus 3:5). God declared to Moses His greatest name, "I am who I am. This is what you are to say to the Israelites: I AM has sent me to you" (Exodus 3:14 NIV). Dear friend, will you, like Moses, turn aside to look at the burning bush, remove your sandals, and walk on this most holy ground? Then like Moses, you will discover with reverence the personal name of God—*Yahweh.*

DISCOVER YAHWEH

When God revealed His name, *I AM WHO I AM,* He spoke His name using Hebrew verbs, not nouns. The verb forms are in the imperfect tense, implying continuing, unfinished action: "I am the one who always is." *Yahweh* is often called the *tetragrammaton* or "four-lettered name"; the Hebrew word translated "I AM" is *YHWH,* transliterated *Yahweh. Yahweh* is so sacred a word in rabbinical writings that it is distinguished with euphemistic expressions such as "the name," "the unutterable name," and "the holy name." Jewish reverence for *Yahweh* is so great that authors and writers frequently refrained from putting the name into print or speaking the name aloud.[1] Perhaps most telling, *Yahweh* is used 6823 times in the Old Testament alone and is rendered *LORD,* usually in small capital letters, befitting its sacred and personal nature.

In San Diego, I had the great opportunity to view a comprehensive exhibition of the Qumran Dead Sea Scrolls, originally discovered between 1947 and 1956. The Dead Sea Scrolls date from 250 BC to AD 68 and include some 230 manuscripts representing nearly every book in the Old Testament. Only when I came upon a certain scroll known as the *Testimonia,* found in cave 4, did I truly appreciate the awe and reverence due to the name and transliteration *Yahweh.*

I stood before a glass case containing the *Testimonia* fragment. At first it seemed innocuous enough, one scroll among many, this scroll with only five disparate verses from the Bible, all on the subject of the Messiah. I had already peered into 15 such cases and respectfully viewed their scrolls. But I guess I had not really seen. Staring at the first line from the verse in Deuteronomy, I got to the place where the Hebrew letters for Yahweh should be written. But instead there were only four dots. I suddenly realized that the reverence of these scribes prohibited them from even putting ink to paper to write the letters *YHWH.* The holiness of God's Word and His name came alive to my heart. Four dots representing all that is Almighty God. I will never view *Yahweh* the same again.

Yahweh *or* Jehovah?

The true pronunciation for YHWH, known to the patriarchs (Genesis 28:13) and Moses (Exodus 3:14), has been lost following the destruction of Jerusalem in AD 70. Because the third commandment in Exodus 20:7 instructed, "You shall not take the name of the LORD your God in vain," the Masorete scribes, working from the seventh to the eleventh centuries AD (and who added a vowel notation system to Hebrew), substituted the vowel marks for *Adonai* under the letters YHWH. This led to a pronunciation of YHWH as *Jehovah*. The shortened form *Yah* is probably part of the original pronunciation (see Psalm 68:4; Isaiah 26:4), but the true pronunciation is unknown. Various proposed pronunciations exist, but current convention by many scholars seems to be the use of the transliteration *Yahweh* for *YHWH*. It is assumed that in this book wherever used, *Yahweh* reverently represents the name *YHWH*.

DRAW NEAR TO YAHWEH

God always works according to His own plan and time frame. With perfect timing, He breaks into history and works in powerful ways in the lives of His people. Perhaps the greatest intervention by God recorded in the Bible (other than the incarnation) is the deliverance of the sons of Israel from Egypt. Though Moses may seem at first glance to be an unlikely servant for this monumental task, God chose him and spoke to him at the burning bush. The first word He said was personal—He spoke Moses' name. And subsequently, "Certainly I will be with you." He knows us by name and calls us by name. His entreaty to Moses was indicative of the intimate relationship He would require for His people: "I will dwell among the sons of Israel and will be their God" (Exodus 29:45).

When Moses heard God call his name, Moses responded, "Here I am" (Exodus 3:4), a natural response, yet a slightly presumptuous one. God gently but firmly reminded Moses of his position, "Remove your sandals" on this "holy ground." However personal and intimate God is with us, He is still God, Creator of the universe, self-existent, ineffable, immutable, holy, and majestic. His very being and presence command sheer reverence, utter respect, and absolute worship. Regardless of how close, personal, or intimate a relationship we have with Him, we must confess that He is "wholly other." He is God, and we are not. And yet He speaks. He invites. He touches. He enters our lives. He initiates. He is insistent and persistent.

I remember standing in the Sistine Chapel in the Vatican, lifting my gaze for a first view of Michelangelo's magnificent rendering of God and Adam. God reaches out His finger with the spark of life toward the outstretched hand of Adam! My first thought was, *Amazing—a personal God—Yahweh!* And to think, my great God chooses to reach out to me and desires a relationship with me.

When Moses suddenly realized who was speaking to him, he hid his face, afraid to look at God. Only then, to a reverent listener, did God pour out His heart to Moses. He had seen the affliction of His people, He had heard their cries, and He was aware of their suffering. Oh, this is such good news for the people of God. You can know that whatever your circumstance, however much you have cried out to God, and wherever your suffering occurs, God sees, He hears, and He knows. And when Yahweh acts, He delivers a definitive response. That, my friend, is the message of Yahweh.

When God revealed His name *Yahweh* to Moses, He was revealing who He is *to* His people and what He does *for* His people. I have included a selective list of attributes of Yahweh's person and works for further study in appendix 2.

Trusting in Jesus as I AM

"Jesus said to them, 'Truly, truly, I say to you, before Abraham was born, I am'" (John 8:58).

John describes a dramatic confrontation between Jesus and the Pharisees in John 8, pointing directly to the deity of the Christ as Yahweh. The Greek for the words "I am" is *ego eimi,* the same Greek words used in the Septuagint (the Greek translation of the Hebrew Old

Testament) for the name *YHWH* or *Yahweh*. Jesus declared for all to hear, "I am." He was proclaiming to those who were standing before Him that He existed before Abraham, was greater than Abraham, and was the same one who had spoken with Moses and delivered His people out of Egypt. He was saying that they were His people, and He was their God. Yahweh was now in their midst as He had promised through Zechariah and the other prophets (Zechariah 2:10; 8:3).

Do you think those who heard the words of Jesus understood what He was saying? All you need to do is read the response of the religious leaders: "Therefore they picked up stones to throw at Him, but Jesus hid Himself and went out of the temple" (John 8:59). Jesus revealed His identity clearly to His disciples. Philip said to Him, "Lord, show us the Father, and it is enough for us." Jesus said, as only Yahweh can say, "Have I been so long with you, and yet you have not come to know Me, Philip?" (John 14:8-9).

What does knowing Yahweh tell you about yourself? Your deepest needs can be fulfilled only by Yahweh, the *ego eimi,* the I AM. He is your bread of life, who sustains you (John 6:35). He is your light, who shows you truth and causes growth in your life (John 8:12). He is the door, who provides the way to eternal life (John 10:7-9). He is your good shepherd, who gives you security (John 10:11,14). He is the resurrection and the life, who gives you eternal life (John 11:25). He is the way, the truth, and the life, who leads you to salvation and abundant life (John 14:6). He is the true vine, who provides for your every need (John 15:1,5).

DECLARE YAHWEH

What must you do when you embrace the name of Yahweh? You must first remove your sandals, for you must stand reverently on holy ground. Then come humbly: *Yahweh, here I am.* Consider the words of Moses to Yahweh, which reflect their face-to-face relationship (Exodus 33:11): "Now, therefore, I pray You, if I have found favor in Your sight, let me know Your ways that I may know You, so that I may find favor in your sight" (verse 13). Yahweh responded with even greater intimacy, descending in a cloud and passing in front of Moses, proclaiming, "The LORD, the LORD God, compassionate and gracious, slow to anger, and abounding in lovingkindness and truth; who keeps lovingkindness for thousands, who forgives iniquity, transgression, and sin" (Exodus 34:6-7). And your response in kind, with all your mind, heart, and soul, is to make haste, like Moses, and bow low to the ground and worship Him.

Speak to your mind, heart, and soul, saying, *Yahweh is my God. There is none like Him.* What can you say to the world about Yahweh? Think about Yahweh's instructions to Moses in a renewal of the Mosaic covenant and then apply this concept to your own situation. Yahweh told Moses to warn the people not to enter into any covenant with the people around them, or it would become a snare in their midst (Exodus 34:12). In the same way, even today, we are not to love the world. Then Yahweh declared, "You shall not worship any other god, for the LORD, whose name is Jealous is a jealous God" (verse 14). Encourage those around you to love Yahweh, live for Yahweh and, as Tozer used to say, "follow hard" after Him. Love the Lord your God with all your heart, soul, mind, and strength. This is the greatest commandment and the greatest declaration you can make to the world.

DEPEND ON YAHWEH

Can you remember the day when you fully realized God wanted you to be in an intimate relationship with Him? What was your response? I'll tell you mine. After I surrendered my life to the Lord Jesus in college, I regularly attended a campus Bible study. One night a guest lecturer, an astronomer, presented a dazzling array of slides on God and the creation of the universe. Later that night, arriving home, I got out of my car and stared into the night sky. Suddenly, seeing all those stars, my heart pressed into my chest, I was overcome with emotion as I sensed the overwhelming presence of God. I ran into the house and into my room, threw myself onto the bed, and covered my head with my pillow. Still, I could not get away from Him.

I have never forgotten the majestic fullness of His presence I experienced that night. To be honest, I rarely share this experience because it was so precious and meaningful to me—the kind of intimacy that is private and personal between Yahweh and me. And I don't want to be misunderstood:

We are never to seek an experience. We must be firmly grounded in God's Word and walk by faith in what He says. But sometimes God seems to "turn down the volume" of His glory, as He did passing in front of Moses, so you can realize His greatness and glory. Worship, then, is your first and primary act of trust and dependence.

Another act of dependence on your part is to pursue Yahweh. Knowing Yahweh makes you realize your need for Him. Because He is the source of meaning, purpose, and ultimate satisfaction in all of life, He is the one who takes top spot on your agenda. There is no greater time of the day than the private, personal, intimate quiet time you spend alone with Yahweh. Step away from everything else in life and draw near to Him, listen to what He says to you in His Word, and talk with Him about everything that is on your heart.

Learn to run to Yahweh in every circumstance of your life. Yahweh has all the answers and holds the keys to everything you face. He is not worried. He is not surprised. He is not wondering what He is going to do. He delights that you confidently run to Him. And as a result of your act of dependence, you will love and enjoy Yahweh. He loves you. Nothing can separate you from His love. Remember, He is always with you, and He will never leave you or forsake you.

DELIGHT IN YAHWEH

A.W. Tozer used to say that if new Christians would meditate on the words of the Bible and the hymns of Watts and Wesley, they would indeed become fine theologians. One of my favorite hymns of Wesley, "And Can It Be That I Should Gain," expresses the delight of a heart that is fully reverential and submissive and that comprehends the sovereign deliverance of Yahweh. Meditate on the words of this hymn when you want to delight in the name of Yahweh.

> And can it be that I should gain
> An interest in the Savior's blood?
> Died He for me, who caused His pain—
> For me, who Him to death pursued?
> Amazing love! How can it be,

That Thou, my God, shouldst die for me?

'Tis mystery all: th'Immortal dies:
Who can explore His strange design?
In vain the firstborn seraph tries
To sound the depths of love divine.
'Tis mercy all! Let earth adore,
Let angel minds inquire no more.

He left His Father's throne above
So free, so infinite His grace—
Emptied Himself of all but love,
And bled for Adam's helpless race:
'Tis mercy all, immense and free,
For O my God, it found out me!

Long my imprisoned spirit lay,
Fast bound in sin and nature's night;
Thine eye diffused a quickening ray—
I woke, the dungeon flamed with light;
My chains fell off, my heart was free,
I rose, went forth, and followed Thee.

No condemnation now I dread;
Jesus, and all in Him, is mine;
Alive in Him, my living Head,
And clothed in righteousness divine,
Bold I approach th'eternal throne,
And claim the crown, through Christ my own.

My Response

DATE:

KEY VERSE: "God said to Moses, 'I am who I am. This is what you are to say to the Israelites: I AM has sent me to you'" (Exodus 3:14 NIV).

FOR FURTHER THOUGHT: What is the most important truth you have learned about Yahweh? How does knowing Him inspire a great faith and devotion to Him? What is your response to Him? How will you trust in Yahweh today?

MY RESPONSE:

Day Twenty-One

TRUSTING IN YAHWEH ROPHE—HE IS YOUR HEALER

I, the LORD, am your healer.
EXODUS 15:26

Trusting in Yahweh Rophe brings healing to your life. We face many trials and afflictions—physical, emotional, and spiritual infirmities. Yahweh Rophe, the Lord your healer, is the object of your trust. He is your comfort in such desperate times. God chose to reveal Himself to Moses as Yahweh Rophe during a time of bitterness. The people of Israel had traveled from the Red Sea three days into the wilderness of Shur without water. The people grumbled, Moses prayed, and the Lord made the bitter waters of Marah sweet so the people could quench their thirst. Following that trial, the Lord told the people, "I, the LORD, am your healer" (Exodus 15:26). When you encounter bitter waters, do you complain the way the people of Israel did, or do you cry out to the Lord, following Moses' example? What will help you, in the most intense times of pain, to cry out to the Lord? Knowing Yahweh Rophe, the Lord your healer.

DISCOVER YAHWEH ROPHE

The Hebrew phrase translated "the LORD who heals" is *Yahweh Rophe* and reveals God's ability to restore, to heal, and to cure, not only in the physical sense but also in the moral and spiritual sense.[1] The Hebrew root verb *rapha* ("to heal") occurs approximately 70 times in the Old Testament.

DRAW NEAR TO YAHWEH ROPHE

God gave His name *Yahweh Rophe* to Moses and the people of Israel during the journey from Egypt to the promised land. They had miraculously crossed the divided Red Sea, fleeing the pursuing Egyptians. Then "the people feared the LORD, and they believed in the LORD and in His servant Moses" (Exodus 14:31). Celebrating this great victory, they sang a song of praise to the Lord: "The LORD shall reign forever and ever" (Exodus 15:18).

But how quickly they forgot the Lord's power. When they had traveled for three days into the wilderness of Shur and found no water, they finally came to the waters of Marah, but they could not drink for the water was bitter. Desperate because of their thirst, they grumbled and complained to Moses. Moses cried out to the Lord, who instructed him to throw a tree into the water, making it sweet and safe to drink.

We learn that God used this event to test the people of Israel (Exodus 15:25). And how often is a bitter difficulty or discouragement a test of our own faith? How often does an event in our lives cause us to wonder, *Can God help me?* In all the bitterness you face in life, always remember God's names. As Yahweh Rophe, the Lord who heals, God changed the waters from bitter to sweet for the people of Israel, and so He can change your pain and disappointment, giving you a new view of God Himself so that you may trust Him more.

We experience healing every day of our lives, and most of the time, our healing goes unnoticed and unrecognized. What of our body's immune cells that travel our bloodstream every day in constant surveillance for potential cancer cells? What of the continual restoration and repair of our cell membranes, blood vessel walls, and organ systems? How often does God use the hands of earthly physicians in His healing work? How many times has an antibiotic helped to destroy an infection?

When all is said and done, what actually healed the infection, repaired the cells, or restored a bodily process? I believe it is none other than the divine work of Yahweh Rophe, for God Himself created the amazing design of the human body and its ability to fight off diseases and infections every day of our lives. God even heals the brokenhearted (Psalm 147:3) and uses His Word to heal and deliver His people (Psalm 107:20). What's more, God heals, restores, and comforts unconditionally, in spite of our own actions (Isaiah 57:18).

Trusting in Jesus as Your Healer

"And the book of the prophet Isaiah was handed to Him, and He opened the book and found the place where it was written, 'The Spirit of the LORD is upon me...He has sent me to proclaim release to the captives, and recovery of sight to the blind' " (Luke 4:17-18).

Jesus closed the book He had read from, sat down, and said to all in the synagogue at Nazareth, "Today this Scripture has been fulfilled in your hearing" (verse 21). What a marvelous declaration of the healing ministry of Jesus! The description of the Messiah in Isaiah 53:3-5 includes healing by His scourging, the bearing of our griefs, and the carrying of our sorrows. The Gospels record the healings of Jesus—casting out demons (Luke 4:33), eliminating a high fever (Luke 4:39), healing leprosy (Luke 5:15), and raising a paralytic (Luke 5:25). Spiritual, physical, and emotional healing came by the hands of Jesus, who said, "It is not those who are healthy who need a physician, but those who are sick; I did not come to call the righteous but sinners" (Mark 2:17). All who were sick were coming to Him, and "He was healing them" (Luke 4:40). In eternity, our blessed assurance is that all who belong to Christ will be healed completely and never experience pain or sickness again (Revelation 21:4). Amen!

What does knowing Yahweh Rophe tell you about yourself? You need His healing touch in your life. The story is told of a mansion in northern Scotland that had been newly decorated and painted. Following the remodel of the mansion, a bottle of soda water exploded, staining the walls with dark splotches. A great artist happened to be visiting at the time. To everyone's amazement, the artist took a simple piece of charcoal, and with a few well-placed strokes, he transformed the walls into a magnificent artistic master-piece. What a picture of the healing touch of Yahweh Rophe, whose touch can bring color and beauty even to the worst pain and disfigurement.

Declare Yahweh Rophe

Are you in need of healing today? Do you have a broken heart, a wounded soul, or a physical illness or disability? Declare the name of Yahweh Rophe and take your need to Him with the words of the psalmist: "Be gracious to me, O Lord, for I am pining away; heal me, O Lord, for my bones are dismayed. And my soul is greatly dismayed; but You, O Lord—how long? Return, O Lord, rescue my soul; save me because of Your loving-kindness" (Psalm 6:2-4). Pray the prayer of Jeremiah. "Heal me, O Lord, and I will be healed. Save me and I will be saved" (Jeremiah 17:14). Then, say to your mind, heart, and soul, "He heals the brokenhearted and binds up their wounds" (Psalm 147:3). *Someday He will wipe every tear from my eyes; and there will no longer be any death; there will no longer be any mourning, or crying, or pain* (Revelation 21:4). And finally, declare to the world, "The Lord is your healer."

Depend on Yahweh Rophe

Trusting God does not mean telling God anything. Trusting means relying on God's names and then waiting patiently to see what He will accomplish. Remember, TRUST means Total Reliance Under Stress and Trial. Can God heal? Yes. Will He heal? Yes, He is Yahweh Rophe. The Lord is the Great Physician. But how and when will He heal? We cannot presume to know. Watch and wait to see how He heals. And trust your Yahweh Rophe.

Sometimes His healing is within your heart, strengthening you to face your difficulty with a new endurance. Annie Johnson Flint suffered crippling arthritis and lived in a wheelchair her entire life. Did she not trust enough? When you read her poetry, you discover a rare heart that trusted the Lord more than most. Her strength in her Lord enabled her to endure the daily pain and life in her wheelchair.

I think of her often because of my own mother's daily suffering with multiple sclerosis and life in a wheelchair. God has not healed my mother physically, but He has offered her and our whole family tremendous spiritual and emotional healing. I have a friend, diagnosed with a brain tumor, who ran to Yahweh Rophe for physical healing. I have another friend whose mother suffered seven years with Alzheimer's disease. I just received an e-mail from one of her relatives, giving me the news that my friend's mother is now face-to-face with her Lord. Another friend's husband who suffered debilitating effects of a massive stroke is also now with the Lord. Our ultimate healing will come when we are with our Lord in eternity.

The story is told of a world conqueror leading his victorious army back to their home in Italy. They marched across rugged terrain and came to the base of the Alps. As they climbed and hiked through the treacherous mountain passes, they became discouraged by the difficulty of the climb, thinking they would never reach home. The great general shouted to his men, "Beyond those Alps lies Italy!" Their hearts revived, they pressed on toward their goal, and finally they reached home.[2] Dear friend, beyond the mountains of difficulty and obstacles you endure in this life is a beautiful land, your eternal home, heaven, where we will finally be free from the presence of death, mourning, crying, and pain (Revelation 21:4).

DELIGHT IN YAHWEH ROPHE

Use the words of the psalmist to delight in Yahweh Rophe:

> Praise the LORD! For it is good to sing praises to our God; for it is pleasant and praise is becoming. The LORD builds up Jerusalem; He gathers the outcasts of Israel. He heals the brokenhearted and binds up their wounds. He counts the number of the stars; He gives names to all of them. Great is our Lord and abundant in strength; His understanding is infinite. The LORD supports the afflicted (Psalm 147:1-6).

My Response

DATE:

KEY VERSE: "I, the LORD, am your healer" (Exodus 15:26).

FOR FURTHER THOUGHT: How does knowing Yahweh Rophe bring hope and comfort to you? What do you need from Him today? What will you ask the one who holds you in His hand?

MY RESPONSE:

Day Twenty-Two

TRUSTING IN YAHWEH NISSI—HE IS YOUR VICTORY

Moses built an altar and named it The LORD is My Banner.
Exodus 17:15

Trusting in Yahweh Nissi gives you confidence in every struggle. Surely in the heat of the battle you need confidence to prevail. Your confidence comes from the assurance of victory from God, who fights for you. Moses discovered the secret of victory when he and the people of Israel were attacked by the armies of Amalek. This was the second real challenge following their Red Sea deliverance. "So Joshua overwhelmed Amalek and his people with the edge of the sword" (Exodus 17:13). Following this victory, God revealed Himself again with a new name, *Yahweh Nissi.* "Moses built an altar and named it The LORD My Banner" (Exodus 17:15). Who can you rely on when you face a spiritual battle with seemingly insurmountable opposition? Run to Yahweh Nissi—He is your victory.

DISCOVER YAHWEH NISSI

The Hebrew phrase translated "The LORD is My Banner" is *Yahweh Nissi*. Historically, another rendering by authors and scholars has been *Jehovah Nissi,* although, as we discussed on day 20, the preferred rendering is *Yahweh Nissi. Yahweh Nissi* is only used once in the Old Testament, here in Exodus 17:15.

DRAW NEAR TO YAHWEH NISSI

What did God intend for Moses, the people of Israel, and subsequent believers to understand from the revelation of Himself as Yahweh Nissi? The conclusion calls for perspective. The people of Israel, led by Moses, faced many challenges on their journey from Egypt to the promised land. They were chased by the Egyptians, crossed the Red Sea, experienced hunger and thirst, and quarreled among themselves about whether God was really with them (Exodus 17:7).

Lack of water soon became the least of their worries. As soon as their thirst was quenched with the water from a rock, they were attacked by Amalek, the chief of an Edomite tribe and a warrior descendant of Esau. Moses commissioned Joshua to lead the battle as Moses stationed himself on the top of a hill with the staff of God in his hand. When Moses held up his hands high, Israel prevailed in the battle, but when his hands fell, Amalek would prevail. When Aaron and Hur helped support Moses' arms high into the air, the victory was won.

Yahweh instructed Moses to record this experience in a book as a memorial, including His resolve to "utterly blot out the memory of Amalek from under heaven" (Exodus 17:14). Following the Lord's words, Moses built an altar and named it "The LORD is My Banner." The significance of the victory was not lost on Moses. Moses fully realized God as Yahweh Nissi, and it was Yahweh Nissi—not Moses, Joshua, and not the people—who was the real victor in the battle.

Banners were not foreign to the people of Israel and were often attached to bare poles or standards. Holding a banner "was a signal to God's people to rally to Him. It stood for His cause, His battle."[1] The banner represented deliverance and salvation. When Moses held up his hands, the people of Israel relied on God for their assurance and their victory.

Though God is called *Yahweh Nissi* only once in the Bible, His work is seen throughout Scripture. We learn that the Lord will fight for us, the battle is His, and He is a God of deliverances (Exodus 14:14; Deuteronomy 3:22; 1 Samuel 17:47; Psalm 68:20). Jeremiah said that Yahweh was with him like a "dread champion" (Jeremiah 20:11). David described Yahweh's spectacular response when he called out to Him in his distress—a sure sign that the Lord was his banner. The Lord heard David's voice:

> Then the earth shook and quaked; and the foundations of the mountains were trembling and were shaken, because He was angry. Smoke went up out of His nostrils, and fire from His mouth…He rode upon a cherub and flew; and He sped upon the wings of the wind…the LORD also thundered in the heavens, and the Most High uttered His voice…He sent out His arrows, and scattered them, and lightning flashes in abundance, and routed them…He sent from on high, He took me; He drew me out of many waters. He delivered me from my strong enemy, and from those who hated me, for they were too mighty for me. They confronted me in the day of my calamity, but the LORD was my stay. He brought me forth also into a broad place; He rescued me, because He delighted in me (Psalm 18:6-19).

The next time you are in desperate trouble, call out to Yahweh Nissi and remind yourself of these words of David in Psalm 18! What a victory you will experience with the Lord as your banner!

What does knowing Yahweh Nissi tell you about yourself? You need someone to fight for you and bring victory in your life. The Lord is the one who fights for you. Run to Yahweh Nissi when you need victory in the battle you face today. What will the banner of the Lord look like in your life? Some scholars suggest that Moses' upraised hands represented prayers and petitions and intercession on behalf of the people of God in the heat of the battle.[2] David mentions banners in the context of God's saving strength:

> We will sing for joy over your victory, and in the name of our God we will set up our banners. May the LORD fulfill all your petitions. Now I know that the LORD saves His anointed; He will answer him from His holy heaven with the saving strength

of His right hand. Some boast in chariots and some in horses, but we will boast in the name of the LORD, our God (Psalm 20:5-7).

Prayer raises the banner of Yahweh Nissi in the midst of any battle.

Trusting in Jesus as Your Victory

"Finally, be strong in the Lord and in the strength of His might" (Ephesians 6:10).

Why do we need this encouragement from Paul to find strength in the Lord? Because we are in a spiritual battle. Our enemies are the world, flesh, and the devil (Ephesians 6:11; 1 John 2:14-15). You can take courage, however, because "greater is He who is in you than he who is in the world" (1 John 4:4). And then, always remember the words of the bride for her beloved, thought to be a picture of Christ and the church: "His banner over me is love" (Song of Solomon 2:4). Love is a great standard to hold high—it is the standard of Christ, and we must always remember that "love never fails" (1 Corinthians 13:8), that "we overwhelmingly conquer through Him Who loved us" (Romans 8:37), and that we can never be separated from "the love of God, which is in Christ Jesus our Lord" (Romans 8:38-39).

DECLARE YAHWEH NISSI

When you recognize you are in a battle, the very first thing you must do is run to Yahweh Nissi, holding His banner high, crying out, *Yahweh Nissi, You are my Banner. The battle is Yours. You are my dread champion. The victory is Yours.* Say to your mind, heart, and soul, *The Lord my God is the one fighting for me. He will send from on high, take me, and draw me out of many waters. He is my stay and can bring me forth into a broad place.* Finally, what shall you declare to the world in your battle? "Greater is He who is in me than he who is in the world!" God is greater, and He will win the victory.

DEPEND ON YAHWEH NISSI

What banner do you carry in life? Is Yahweh Nissi your banner? Or do you carry the banner of self, believing you are the only one to fight the battle? Or do you carry the banner of money, believing if only you could be a millionaire, you could win your war? Or is the banner of position your reliance, believing if only you could have the perfect job, your problem, whatever it may be, will be solved?

When you are in the heat of the battle, think of Moses and the staff in his hand. When he held the staff high, Israel won, and when it fell, they began to lose. And so it is with you—defeat is sure if you hold up any banner but Yahweh Nissi. Victory is certain if you hold high your banner, Yahweh Nissi. Look to the Lord to fight your battles. Cry out to Him. The Lord will give you wisdom every step of the way as He leads you.

Joshua and the people still fought with the sword, but Yahweh Nissi, the Lord their Banner, went before them, fought for them, and won the victory. Always remind yourself, "Greater is He who is in you than he who is in the world." And then carry the banner of love. "Walk in love, just as Christ also loved you and gave Himself up for us" (Ephesians 5:2). The sacrificial life of love has won many a battle that could never be conquered with harsh words, and provides, according to Paul, the perfect bond of unity (Colossians 3:14).

Pray in the heat of the battle and watch the Lord win the battle—He is victor. Hudson Taylor tells the remarkable story of how his rebellion in his teen years drove his mother and younger sister to fervent prayer on his behalf. After his seventeenth birthday, his mother spent two weeks at a friend's home 70 miles away. One afternoon after lunch, his mother went to her room, locked the door, and got down on her knees to pray for her son's conversion to Christ. She resolved she would not stop until she was assured the battle was won. She prayed for hours until she could pray no more. She became convinced that the victory had been won and her son would trust in Christ.

That same afternoon, at home alone, Hudson became bored and ventured into his father's study, searching for a book to read. A gospel tract captured his attention, and he picked it up, thinking he might find a good story. He curled up in the corner of the room and began reading, fully intending to stop if he came to any religious parts. But he read one phrase he could not get out of his mind: "the finished work of Christ." Then the words of Christ on the cross came to His mind: "It is finished." His struggle with religion had been that he could not seem to produce enough good works to outweigh his bad deeds, so he just gave up trying. Now, a new question came to his mind: *What was finished?* Suddenly, he realized the truth—the debt of his sin had been paid in full by Christ. He fell on his knees and received Christ as His Savior.

At that very moment, his mother had ceased praying, assured by God that her son would come to Christ. She arrived home six days later. He excitedly met her at the door and said, "Mother, I have some happy news for you!" She hugged him and said, "I know, my boy. I've been rejoicing for days in the glad tiding you have to tell me." Oh, what a victory was won by the Lord in the spiritual battle for the soul of Hudson Taylor, who went on to become the founder of the China Inland Mission, bringing thousands of souls to Christ in China.

DELIGHT IN YAHWEH NISSI

Oh, how exciting to watch Yahweh Nissi gain the victory in a life, whether that life is your own, a family member's, or a friend's. Joy is your great response in praising Yahweh Nissi. Nehemiah taught the people of God, "The joy of the LORD is your strength" (Nehemiah 8:10). How can you rejoice in Him today? Praise Him with the words of the psalmist. You can move from one psalm to the next and discover how to praise, rejoice in, and worship the Lord. I especially love the words of Psalm 111:1-3: "Praise the LORD! I will give thanks to the LORD with all my heart, in the company of the upright and in the assembly. Great are the works of the LORD; they are studied by all who delight in them. Splendid and majestic is His work, and His righteousness endures forever."

My Response

DATE:

KEY VERSE: "Moses built an altar and named it The Lord is My Banner" (Exodus 17:15).

FOR FURTHER THOUGHT: Describe what it means to know and trust Yahweh Nissi. What is the most important truth you learned today? How do you need Yahweh Nissi in your life?

MY RESPONSE:

Day Twenty-Three

TRUSTING IN YAHWEH MEKADDESH—HE MAKES YOU HOLY

But as for you, speak to the sons of Israel,
saying, "You shall surely observe My sabbaths;
for this is a sign between Me and you
throughout your generations, that you may
know that I am the LORD who sanctifies you."

EXODUS 31:13

Trusting in Yahweh Mekaddesh sets you apart for a revolutionary way of life—holy and sacred living. The current culture certainly knows very little of the truly holy and sacred, as evidenced on every page of any daily newspaper. The holy and sacred is distinct and noticeable. Yahweh Mekaddesh separates you from the crowd—He makes you shine like a light in the world. The Lord revealed His name *Yahweh Mekaddesh* in the context of instructing Moses about the observation of Sabbaths as a sign between Him and His people. He said, "You shall surely observe My sabbaths; for this is a sign between Me and you throughout your generations, that you may know that I am the LORD who sanctifies you" (Exodus

31:13). How can you live a holy and sacred life that pleases the Lord? Yahweh Mekaddesh does for His people what they cannot do for themselves—He sanctifies them.

DISCOVER YAHWEH MEKADDESH

The Hebrew words translated "the LORD who sanctifies" are *Yahweh Mekaddesh* and are first used in Exodus 31:13. The Hebrew verb *kadash*, "to be holy, sanctified, separate," is found most commonly in Leviticus. The words *sanctify* or *be holy* occur in various forms throughout the Old Testament at least 700 times.[1]

DRAW NEAR TO YAHWEH MEKADDESH

Knowing Yahweh Mekaddesh and trusting Him enables you to experience the life you were meant to live. Sanctification follows redemption. We see this in the lives of the people of Israel, and in their example, we have a picture of what God has done in our lives. After the people of Israel were rescued and set free by God from the cruel bondage of Egypt, they began their journey with God. God wanted to be their God, and they were to be His people (Exodus 6:7). He had in mind for them a life with Him in the promised land. What would that mean for these people? They must be sanctified—holy and separate, like their God and not like the surrounding nations.

We first see God revealing Himself as Yahweh Mekaddesh, the Lord who sanctifies, when he instructed His people to observe the Sabbath day. His instruction was given for the purpose of knowing His name. And knowing He was the Lord who sanctifies would remind them of the kind of people they were—His people—holy, set apart, giving Him great glory.

God gave the law to Moses, outlined in Leviticus, so His people would know how to live. In Leviticus, we see that Yahweh Mekaddesh sanctifies with purpose, influencing many areas of life, including keeping the Sabbath (Exodus 31:13), obedience (Leviticus 20:8), holiness (Leviticus 21:7-8), service to God (Leviticus 21:15), health (Leviticus 21:23), eating (Leviticus 22:8-9,16), speech (Leviticus 22:32), and witnessing to the world (Ezekiel 37:28). Notice that God's care and concern for His people's conduct extended to every area of their lives. Here we begin to see the expression of one of God's attributes—His holiness.

As we draw near to Yahweh Mekaddesh, we must contemplate the holiness of God. Merely saying God is different from our culture is not adequate when describing Yahweh Mekaddesh—He is wholly other and separate from all creation. R.C. Sproul defines *holy* as "separate," derived from an ancient word meaning "to cut" and perhaps signifying "a cut above something."[2] A.W. Tozer describes holiness this way:

> Holy is the way God is. To be holy He does not conform to a standard. He is that standard. He is absolutely holy with an infinite, incomprehensible fullness of purity that is incapable of being other than it is. Because He is holy, His attributes are holy; that is, whatever we think of as belonging to God must be thought of as holy.[3]

We are given glimpses into visions of the holiness of God in two throne room scenes in the Bible, one in Isaiah and one in Revelation. When Isaiah saw the Lord, he saw and heard the holiness of God. He saw the Lord "sitting on a throne, lofty and exalted, with the train of His robe filling the temple" (Isaiah 6:1). The seraphim above the Lord called out to one another, "Holy, Holy, Holy, is the LORD of hosts, the whole earth is full of His glory." In this scene we see that His presence fills the room with holiness and glory.

Now, imagine you are able to gain an even larger view of the throne room of God. Revelation 4 takes us to God's throne room in heaven, where we see a rainbow encircling the throne and a sea of glass in front of the throne. Surrounding the throne are 24 elders and four living creatures who worship God. Day and night, the creatures never stop saying, "Holy, holy, holy is the Lord God Almighty who was, and is, and is to come." Then the elders fall down before the Lord who is on the throne and worship Him, casting their crowns before the throne and saying, "You are worthy, our Lord and God, to receive glory and honor and power, for you created all things, and by your will they were created and have their being" (Revelation 4:11 NIV). In these throne room scenes the overwhelming impression is of God's holiness and the utter honor, worship, and attention from all in His presence.

Trusting in Jesus as Your Sanctification

"But by His doing you are in Christ Jesus, who became to us wisdom from God, and righteousness, and sanctification, and redemption" (1 Corinthians 1:30).

God's holiness commands holiness in the lives of His people. We, as New Testament Christians, have experienced a much greater rescue than the people of Israel experienced in the Old Testament. God has "rescued us from the domain of darkness and brought us into the kingdom of the Son he loves, in whom we have redemption, the forgiveness of sins" (Colossians 1:13-14 NIV). And now we are to be holy, for He is holy (1 Peter 1:16). How is it possible for us to be holy? God is Yahweh Mekaddesh, the Lord who sanctifies us.

When you become a Christian, receiving Christ as your Lord and Savior, you become "a new creation; the old has gone, the new has come!" (2 Corinthians 5:17 NIV). He sanctifies you and sets you apart through His indwelling Holy Spirit (Romans 8:9; 1 Corinthians 1:30; Hebrews 10:10-14). You may be thinking, *But I struggle with living a holy life.* Sanctification is not only a singular work accomplished by Christ on the cross but also an ongoing process accomplished by Christ through the power of the Holy Spirit in you (2 Corinthians 3:18; Hebrews 10:14). You now belong to God and you are a temple of the Holy Spirit (1 Corinthians 6:19).

What does knowing Yahweh Mekaddesh tell you about yourself? You are to live a holy life and shine as a light in this world. Remember that you belong to God. As a member of the church, you are part of the bride of Christ. Paul tells us that Christ loved the church so much that He gave Himself up for her (that includes you). He made His sacrifice for a purpose—that He might "sanctify her, having cleansed her by the washing of water with the word, that He might present to Himself the church in all her glory, having no spot or wrinkle or any such thing; but that she would be holy and blameless" (Ephesians 5:25-27).

I will never forget preparing for my wedding to David, my dear husband.

The wedding took place in a single day, but the marriage continues until we are face-to-face with our Lord. The beautiful truth is that your life with the Lord begins now, and you experience it daily as you walk with Him in the strength and power of the Holy Spirit.[4] My husband surprised me with a beautiful diamond anniversary ring for our twenty-fifth wedding anniversary. The diamonds sparkle when the sun shines on them. But what I love most is what that ring represents—I belong to my husband, and he is mine.

And that is how it is with you. When the Son shines on you, the brilliance of His glory sparkles from within your heart, making you distinct and showing the world that you belong to Him. Your holy and sacred life, produced by Christ in you, shines like an anniversary ring, reminding you of all He has been to you over the years, and looks forward to the day when you will stand before Him, beautifully dressed as His bride (Revelation 21:2 NIV).

DECLARE YAHWEH MEKADDESH

Living in a fallen world that is more and more godless with each passing day is a challenge for anyone who loves Jesus Christ. Obedience to God and trust in Him sometimes become difficult and may even seem impossible. Those are the days when you draw near to Yahweh Mekaddesh and say, *You are the Lord who sanctifies me.* Then speak the words Jesus taught us:

> Our Father who is in heaven, hallowed be Your name. Your kingdom come. Your will be done, on earth as it is in heaven. Give us this day our daily bread. And forgive us our debts, as we also have forgiven our debtors. And do not lead us into temptation but deliver us from evil. For Yours is the kingdom and the power and the glory forever. Amen (Matthew 6:9-13).

Say to your own mind, heart, and soul as a reminder of who you are, *I am a member of the bride of Christ. I've been bought with a price, and He has given me His indwelling Holy Spirit as a guarantee of the life that is to come. He is at work in me both to will and work for His good pleasure, and that which He has begun, He will complete. Someday soon, I will see my Lord face-to-face in glory.* Finally, to the world, which is passing away, you can declare the words of the four living creatures in the Revelation 4 throne room scene, who cry out day and night, "Holy, holy, holy is the Lord God Almighty who was, and is, and is to come."

DEPEND ON YAHWEH MEKADDESH

What will help you grow in your relationship with your Lord and experience His sanctifying work in your life? He has given you a magnificent gift in the Bible. Jesus prayed for His disciples, "Sanctify them in the truth; Your word is truth." Living in His Word is one of the great secrets to sanctification, well-known to those who have walked with God. Paul told his disciple Timothy that "all Scripture is inspired by God and profitable for teaching, for reproof, for correction, for training in righteousness; so that the man of God may be adequate, equipped for every good work" (2 Timothy 3:16-17).

Your time with God in His Word will cause you to form convictions that guide your steps, not out of legalism, but out of love for your Lord. The Word of God is alive, and the Spirit of God uses it to transform you from the inside out, making you more and more like Christ. The character of Christ is the fruit of your sanctification—when you grow, you manifest the character qualities of love, joy, peace, patience, kindness, goodness, faithfulness, gentleness, and self-control (Galatians 5:22). You will live a life worthy of the calling you received, influencing everyone and everything around you.

God sets you apart for His purposes—for life with Him, praise, worship, and ministry. Paul describes this transforming, sanctifying work of the Spirit: "We all, with unveiled face, beholding as in a mirror the glory of the Lord, are being transformed into the same image from glory to glory, just as from the Lord, the Spirit" (2 Corinthians 3:18). We become like the one we spend time with and look at the most. When we live our days looking at Jesus, first with quiet time and then throughout the day as we enjoy His presence moment by moment, we cannot help but experience the sanctifying work of our Yahweh Mekaddesh, the Lord who sanctifies us.

DELIGHT IN YAHWEH MEKADDESH

Your delight in Yahweh Mekaddesh is your response to His holiness. Think about what it would be for you to gaze into the throne room of God, the throne encircled by a rainbow, God's train filling the temple, a glassy sea in front of the throne, heavenly creatures crying out, "Holy, holy, holy," and 24 elders casting their crowns before the throne. When Isaiah saw the Lord, he said, "Woe to me!...I am a man of unclean lips, and I live among a people of unclean lips, and my eyes have seen the King, the LORD Almighty" (Isaiah 6:5 NIV). But then we see the action of the Lord who sanctifies as one of the seraphs flies to the disheartened Isaiah with a live coal, touches his mouth, and says, "See, this has touched your lips; your guilt is taken away and your sin atoned for" (Isaiah 6:6-7 NIV).

Imagine the feelings of Isaiah—his utter desperation at his own sin and then his complete exultation at his forgiveness, redemption, sanctification, and glorification. And this, dear friend, is your position as well. You are forgiven, set free, and now set apart for the Lord, that you might live for His glory, holy and separate. May you share in the words of Dick Eastman in *A Celebration of Praise:* "Lord, with my lips I acknowledge Your absolute holiness. You are faultless and undefiled, clean in every way. I praise the totality of Your perfection and purity. You are altogether holy."[5]

My Response

DATE:

KEY VERSE: "You shall surely observe My sabbaths; for this is a sign between Me and you throughout your generations, that you may know that I am the LORD who sanctifies you" (Exodus 31:13).

FOR FURTHER THOUGHT: What impresses you the most about God's holiness? In what area of your life do you need Yahweh Mekaddesh the most today? What have you learned that will help you grow in your relationship with Christ?

MY RESPONSE:

Day Twenty-Four

QUIET TIME WEEK FOUR: TRUSTING GOD AS MOSES DID

Then Moses said, "I pray You,
show me Your glory."

EXODUS 33:18

PREPARE YOUR HEART

In every generation, a few people step out of the crowd and dare to draw near. Their lives are no longer defined by the culture of the day or even the religious mores of their contemporaries. They are transformed and guided by one unseen, the great and glorious God, whose name they have come to know and love and trust. A.W. Tozer was one such man of God in his time. His relationship with God was considered to be so deep that many called him God's prophet for the day, clearly speaking His truth from His Word. He pastored Southside Alliance Church in Chicago for 31 years and was editor of the magazine *The Alliance Weekly*. Most know Tozer for the books he has written about God, especially *The Pursuit of God*, *The Knowledge of the Holy*, and *The Divine Conquest*.

Such knowledge of God as is unveiled in these books could only come from reading the Bible facedown in worship of the God who is revealed in its pages. For only God can make Scripture come alive and display His majesty and holiness. Tozer's books show that he knew God in a depth that few others have known. Why? He dared to draw near. And so must you. You must be like Moses, who dared to ask God, "I pray You, show me Your glory!" (Exodus 33:18). What a bold request! But the request delighted God, and He granted it. For a few moments, He "turned down the lights," so Moses could see His back (Exodus 33:23). And when Moses was granted this new magnificent view of God, he bowed low and worshipped. Today, ask the Lord to give you the kind of heart possessed by Moses and Tozer—a heart that dared to draw near.

READ AND STUDY GOD'S WORD

1. Moses was one of our heroes who trusted in the names of God. He knew God because he possessed a great heart—one that dared to draw near to God and know His name. When you know the name of God, you will trust in Him. Look at the following verses and record what you learn about Moses and his requests of God. Note God's response to each request.

Exodus 3:11-12

Exodus 3:13-14

Exodus 33:11-15

Exodus 33:16-17

Exodus 33:18-23

Exodus 34:5-8

Exodus 34:9-10

2. Describe what you see about the heart of Moses. What did he want from God?

3. Summarize God's response to the requests of Moses.

Adore God in Prayer

What do you seek from God? Write out in your own words your desire to draw near to Him. Then pray the prayer of Moses in Psalm 90:17: "Let the favor of the Lord our God be upon us; and confirm for us the work of our hands; yes, confirm the work of our hands."

Yield Yourself to God

The life of Moses was a much-enduring one. He endured the banishment from palatial surroundings and the most brilliant court then in existence; he endured the forfeiture of privilege, and the renunciation of splendid prospects; he endured the flight from Egypt, and the wrath of the king; he endured the lonely exile in Midian, where for years he was buried alive; he endured the long trudge through the wilderness at the head of a slave people, whom he sought to consolidate into a nation; he endured the ill manners and the countless provocations of a forward and perverse generation; he endured the lonely death on Nebo, and the nameless grave that angels dug for him there! And here we have the secret of his wondrous fortitude disclosed to us: *He endured, as seeing him who is invisible.* He realized the presence of God. He lived in the consciousness, "Thou God seest me." He looked up, and had an habitual regard to the heavenly and eternal. In the upper chambers of his soul there was a window that opened skyward, and commanded a view of things unseen. As an old author puts it, "He had a greater than Pharoah in his eye, and this kept him right." Yes, and this will keep any of us right; to live under the sense that God is overlooking us—to walk by faith and not by sight.[1]

S. Law Wilson

Enjoy His Presence

What have you learned this week from the example of Moses? What is your favorite name of God you learned about this week and why? What name of God means the most to you today?

Rest in His Love

"For he endured as seeing Him who is unseen" (Hebrews 11:27).

Notes—Week Four

DISCOVERING GOD'S CARE AND CONCERN

Days 25–30

Day Twenty-Five

TRUSTING IN
YAHWEH SHALOM—
HE IS YOUR PEACE

But the LORD said to him, "Peace!
Do not be afraid. You are not going to
die." So Gideon built an altar to the LORD
there and called it The LORD is Peace."

JUDGES 6:23-24 NIV

Trusting in Yahweh Shalom gives you a new view of adversity. God has not abandoned you in your trouble. Rather, He may be leading you into a new place of influence. God's peace, given to you by Yahweh Shalom, "The Lord is Peace," will carry you. Consider Gideon, whom the Lord addressed as a "mighty warrior" during the Midianites' attack on Israel. God revealed Himself in a new way to Gideon through His name *Yahweh Shalom.* "Gideon built an altar to the LORD there and called it The LORD is Peace" (Judges 6:23-24 NIV). And in that name, Gideon received a peace so great that he was strengthened to accomplish a great work of God. Gideon, the mighty warrior, had met Yahweh Shalom, and as a result, he experienced the deep and abiding shalom of God. For everything you experience in life, you need shalom. And where can you find this kind of peace? By running to Yahweh Shalom—He is your peace.

DISCOVER YAHWEH SHALOM

The Hebrew phrase translated "The LORD is Peace" is transliterated *Yahweh Shalom* and occurs only once in the Old Testament. Shalom is "a harmony of relationship or a reconciliation passed upon the completion of a transaction, the payment of a debt, the giving of satisfaction."[1] Shalom is the greatest contentment and satisfaction in life. *Shalom* is translated "peace" about 170 times, and derivatives of the Hebrew verb *shalem,* "to be whole, healthy, at peace," occur approximately 400 times in the Bible.

DRAW NEAR TO YAHWEH SHALOM

Two hundred years had passed since the revelation of God as Yahweh Mekaddesh. The people of Israel had forgotten God and were worshipping the gods of the surrounding nations. How did God feel about their idolatry? We are told, "the Israelites did evil in the eyes of the LORD, and for seven years he gave them into the hands of the Midianites" (Judges 6:1 NIV). The Israelites were forced to run for their very lives and hide in the mountains. They could not even plant crops because when they did, the Amalekites and Midianites invaded their land, ruined their crops, and killed their livestock. The people of Israel were so devastated that finally they "cried out to the LORD for help" (Judges 6:6 NIV).

Oh, what a happy day it is when a man or woman of God finally cries to the Lord for help! Psalm 107, thematically similar, describes times of loss, suffering, and adversity for the redeemed of the Lord. It also provides the defining response that turned the tide in each situation—they cried out to the Lord in their trouble. In the midst of difficult days for the people of God, God will often raise up someone who is His man or woman for the hour.

Such was the case with the Israelites when they turned to their God for help. The Lord appeared to Gideon as he was beating out wheat in a winepress, and He said, "The LORD is with you, mighty warrior" (Judges 6:12 NIV).

Gideon resisted, "If the LORD is with us, why then has all this happened to us?" concluding, "The LORD has abandoned us."

But the Lord immediately redirected Gideon's thinking. "Go in the strength you have and save Israel out of Midian's hand. Am I not sending you?" Then God showed Gideon a sign of His presence and gave Gideon His marching orders. "Peace! Do not be afraid. You are not going to die." Gideon, aware he had wrongly interpreted God, built an altar and called it "The LORD is Peace," for the Lord had revealed Himself as Yahweh Shalom.

What difference did Yahweh Shalom make in Gideon's life? His experience with Yahweh Shalom led to boldness and courage in tearing down his own father's idols to Baal and Asherah. Gideon developed a heart of reverence to God, building an altar to God at His instruction. He enjoyed a powerful life of prayer, talking with God through the course of his everyday life. He demonstrated a life of obedience, following God's instructions to defeat the enemies of Israel. He experienced the Spirit of the Lord and fought the enemies of Israel in the strength of the Lord rather than the strength of men. As a result, God used him to lead the people in a powerful victory over their enemies, and they enjoyed peace for 40 years during Gideon's lifetime (Judges 8:28).

Perhaps, my friend, you are plagued with the notion that your God has abandoned you. Learn a lesson from Gideon and the people of Israel. God had not abandoned His people. The very one who thought God had abandoned him was called by God to an even greater calling, to stand and to proclaim his Lord to his generation. And perhaps you, who have thought God has abandoned you, may dimly begin to entertain the perspective that God is calling you to a higher standard—a greater task.

Look at Gideon and believe. Turn to Yahweh Shalom and experience the Lord, who is your peace. Gideon learned that peace was more than a feeling or a state of being, but a person, the Lord Himself, Yahweh Shalom. The peace of God is like a mighty river flowing deep in the heart, strengthening men and women of God to do great and mighty things in the name of their Lord.

Perhaps you have heard the story of the artist who was commissioned by a wealthy man to paint a depiction of peace. He first painted a peaceful country scene and then the serenity of a sleeping baby, but both submissions were rejected by his benefactor. Finally, after much thought, he prayed for an inspired idea from God. Suddenly, the idea came to him; he painted with unrestrained purpose and zeal. When his employer finally studied the finished painting, he looked at the artist and said, "Now this is a picture of true peace." And what was the painting? The fury of a stormy sea striking a rugged cliff. But under the cliff, snuggled safely in its nest, was a small bird, at peace though the stormed raged.

What does knowing Yahweh Shalom tell you about yourself? You need the peace of Yahweh Shalom in your heart. Though the storm rages about you, His peace keeps you secure and calm in Him, trusting His power and strength to pull you through the tempest.

Trusting in Jesus as Your Peace

"Peace I leave with you; My peace I give to you; not as the world gives do I give to you. Do not let your heart be troubled, nor let it be fearful" (John 14:27).

Oh what a matchless gift the peace of God is for the person of God. Perfect peace comes to those who trust in God (Isaiah 26:3). Peace is a blessing from God (Psalm 29:11). We see that Jesus is our peace (Ephesians 2:14) and gives us His peace (John 14:27). His peace is to rule, govern, and control our hearts (Colossians 3:15).

DECLARE YAHWEH SHALOM

When you feel the same way Gideon did, that God has abandoned you, run to Yahweh Shalom and say, *Lord, thank You that You are my peace, that You have a plan, and that You will accomplish what concerns me in my circumstances.* Then, say to your mind, heart, and soul the words that Gideon relied on: "The LORD is with you." Then remind yourself of the words of Jesus, personalizing them for yourself, *The Lord has given me His peace, not as the world gives. I will not be troubled or be afraid* (John 14:27). Perhaps the very best way to declare Yahweh Shalom to the world is to greet any and all with that wonderful word of grace, saying, "Shalom! Peace to you" (see Judges 19:20). And give others the words of Paul: "Now may the Lord of peace Himself continually grant you peace in every circumstance. The Lord be with you all!" (2 Thessalonians 3:16).

DEPEND ON YAHWEH SHALOM

Meeting Yahweh Shalom revolutionized Gideon's relationship with God. When you read about Gideon's life, you will notice that Gideon became a man of prayer. Following the meeting with Yahweh Shalom, Gideon spoke constantly with God, and God talked constantly with Gideon. He lived out the promises of God, "The LORD is with you" and "I will be with you" (Judges 6:12,16). When you become a person of prayer, you will experience the shalom of God. This promise is confirmed in Paul's words, "Be anxious for nothing, but in everything by prayer and supplication with thanksgiving let your requests be made known to God. And the peace of God, which surpasses all comprehension, will guard your hearts and your minds in Christ Jesus" (Philippians 4:6-7).

The Greek word translated "peace" is *eirene:* peace of mind, tranquility, arising from reconciliation with God and a sense of a divine favor.[2] This peace watches over your heart like a guard who watches over a city gate from within. Think about the power of such a guard on your heart. What strength you will have as peace keeps watch over your heart, maintaining your faith, courage, and boldness as you run the race the Lord has set before you. Therefore, whatever your trouble, learn to take it to the Lord in prayer. And then imagine the Lord calming the storm in your heart the same way He calmed the raging waters of the Sea of Galilee when He said, "Peace, be still" (Mark 4:39 KJV). The wind immediately died down and it was completely calm. And so it will be for you when the God of peace brings His shalom to your heart. Alan Redpath says, "If you begin with God, your enemies grow small...get alone somewhere with God until every other voice is silent and all human opinions are shut out, and learn to look to the Lord."[3]

When you pray, you learn. You see the truth, the objective reality, rather than an illusion, created by your earthly perspective. You will discover, like Gideon, that you are not abandoned by God. Instead, you are called by God to be His in a godless and dark world that needs to see He is the one true God.

DELIGHT IN YAHWEH SHALOM

Delighting in Yahweh Shalom will lead you to radiant, rejoicing prayer.

How lovely are the faces of
The men who talk with God—
Lit with an inner sureness of
The path their feet have trod;
How gentle is the manner of
A man who walks with Him!
No strength can overcome him and
No cloud his courage dim.
Keen are the hands and feet—ah yes—
Of those who wait His will,
And clear as crystal mirrors, are
The hearts His love can fill.
Some lives are drear from doubt and fear
While others merely plod;
But lovely faces mark the men
Who walk and talk with God.[4]

PAULINE PROSSER-THOMPSON

DATE:

KEY VERSE: "Gideon built an altar to the LORD there and called it The LORD is Peace" (Judges 6:24).

FOR FURTHER THOUGHT: How does the peace of God help in a time when you may think God has abandoned you? What did you learn from the life of Gideon? In what ways do you need to trust in Yahweh Shalom today?

MY RESPONSE:

TRUSTING IN YAHWEH SABAOTH— HE IS YOUR DELIVERER

Then David said to the Philistine, "You come to me with a sword, a spear, and a javelin, but I come to you in the name of the LORD of hosts, the God of the armies of Israel, whom you have taunted."

1 SAMUEL 17:45

Trusting in Yahweh Sabaoth helps you overcome giants in your life. Do you have an impossible situation? Are you completely without resources? Are you living with a disability or difficulty that has altered your course? How can you face these giants? By trusting in the name of Yahweh Sabaoth, the Lord of hosts. When David encountered the giant Goliath, he said, "You come to me with a sword, a spear, and a javelin, but I come to you in the name of the LORD of hosts, the God of the armies of Israel, whom you have taunted" (1 Samuel 17:45). Are you facing an impossible situation? Run to Yahweh Sabaoth for deliverance and help in your impossibility.

DISCOVER YAHWEH SABAOTH

The Hebrew words translated "the LORD of hosts" are *Yahweh Sabaoth* ("the Lord of the armies") and refer to Yahweh as commander of the armies of heaven and the ruler over all power and might in both heaven and earth. Lockyer says, "Other forces than material, forces unseen and supernatural, multitudes of celestial beings, are at the disposal of Him who is high over all. The whole of His creation is under His control and obeys His sovereign command, willingly or otherwise."[1] *Sabaoth* occurs 250 times in the Old Testament and first appears in 1 Samuel 1:3 in the story of Hannah. The most common occurrences of *Yahweh Sabaoth* are found in the prophets, especially Isaiah (60 times), Jeremiah (60 times), and Zechariah (53 times). These Old Testament believers discovered that Yahweh Sabaoth comes to the aid of His people to help them and deliver them from every giant they face in life.

DRAW NEAR TO YAHWEH SABAOTH

Sometimes the least likely people are ushered into the most holy place of God's names, where they see what others cannot see and experience what others can never experience. Do you feel weak, insignificant, and without resources to face your impossible situation? You are in the exact place where Yahweh Sabaoth can do a mighty work. He reveals Himself especially to the weak and powerless. He delights in delivering those who have no recourse but Him. Paul made it clear that "God has chosen the foolish things of the world to shame the wise, and God has chosen the weak things of the world to shame the things which are strong...so that no man may boast before God" (1 Corinthians 1:27-29). We are to boast in one thing only—the name of the Lord our God (Psalm 20:7).

David was the youngest in his family. While his brothers fought battles in Saul's army, David was sent out to the fields to shepherd the sheep. He was also the errand boy, in charge of delivering provisions to his brothers. But David stood above everyone else in his family because he had a heart for the Lord. He experienced Yahweh and knew Him as the Lord of hosts. He had seen Yahweh deliver him from lions and bears, and he was confident Yahweh Sabaoth would deliver him again.

One day, while bringing supplies to his brothers, David arrived just in time to see the giant Goliath, the Philistine, taunt and challenge the armies of Israel. David watched the armies of Israel flee in terror from Goliath. But David saw life from a different perspective than did the armies of Israel, for he saw only the great affront to the living God. He was incensed that anyone, including Goliath, would even dare to say such things about the Lord. He was also incredulous at the response of Saul's armies. He did not regard them as the armies of Saul, but the armies of the living God (1 Samuel 17:26).

David did not give a second thought to his course of action. He went to King Saul and said, "Let no man's heart fail on account of him; your servant will go and fight with this Philistine." Saul told David that he couldn't possibly fight Goliath because he was only a boy and Goliath had been a warrior since his youth. But David was steadfast in his resolve, unmoved by the words of Saul, for David did not recoil in fear like the armies of Israel or King Saul. He saw Yahweh Sabaoth, the Lord of hosts, and knew Him to be his help and deliverer. David had experienced the Lord of hosts at work, delivering him from danger as he shepherded the sheep. He knew the strength and power of the Lord of hosts, and he knew Yahweh Sabaoth was stronger than Goliath. There was no doubt in his mind.

What did that prior knowledge and godly view accomplish for David? He was confident. He trusted in the name of His God, Yahweh Sabaoth. Wearing no armor, with only a sling and a rock in his hand, he ran out to fight Goliath. Goliath cursed David and told him how he was going to destroy him. Again, David was unmoved by the terrorizing threats of Goliath. David declared, "You come to me with a sword, a spear, and a javelin, but I come to you in the name of the LORD of hosts, the God of the armies of Israel, whom you have taunted" (1 Samuel 17:45). As if that were not enough, David then told Goliath, in explicit detail, exactly how he was going to tear him apart.

Imagine the spectacle. This young boy with no armor is standing in front of a well-armed giant as the Israelite and Philistine armies look on. What an unlikely scene! And isn't that often how you feel when you are in your impossible situation? You have nothing in your hands as you face the giant in your life. And everyone and everything is on the sidelines—you seem to have no one and nothing to help. Ah, but those are only feelings, dear friend. For David was not alone. There was one with him who had, at His command, all the armies of heaven, ready to do battle and fight and deliver. Yahweh Sabaoth, the Lord of hosts, was with David. When the Lord and the armies of heaven stand with you, nothing you face will be too great for you to overcome. Giants are like ants standing before the Lord of hosts and His armies. David took his slingshot, struck Goliath, and cut off Goliath's head with his own sword.

How could a mere boy kill a giant, you ask? The answer: by trusting in the name of Yahweh Sabaoth. And so it has always been true for those who trust in Yahweh Sabaoth. Hannah discovered the power of trusting in Yahweh Sabaoth when she prayed to Him and asked Him to give her a child (1 Samuel 1:11), vowing to dedicate the child to the Lord. Yahweh Sabaoth answered, and she became the mother of Samuel, one of the great prophets of the Lord. Jeremiah discovered, while in exile in Babylon, that there was one who was with him like a dread champion—Yahweh, the Lord of hosts (Jeremiah 20:11-13). In times of trouble and change, the psalmists found comfort in the presence of the Lord of hosts (Psalm 46:11) and blessing from trusting in the Lord of hosts (Psalm 84:12). Isaiah discovered the holiness and glory of the Lord of hosts (Isaiah 6:3; 8:13). He discovered that the Lord of hosts protects and delivers (Isaiah 31:5). Isaiah realized that the one to lean on in difficult times is the Lord of hosts (Isaiah 48:2). And for those who are alone, the Lord of hosts promises to be your Husband, your Maker (Isaiah 54:5). He helps the lonely and delivers the afflicted.

What does knowing Yahweh Sabaoth tell you about yourself? You will face giants in your life, and when you do, run to Yahweh Sabaoth.

Trusting in Jesus as Your Conqueror

"But in all these things we overwhelmingly conquer through Him who loved us" (Romans 8:37).

Jesus encourages us to to take courage in the midst of tribulation, for He has overcome the world. In fact, He accomplished your deliverance when He "reconciled you in His fleshly body through death, in order to present you before Him holy and blameless" (Colossians 1:22). Jesus is the overcomer and will give us strength in our difficulties. Paul cried out, "I can do all things through Him who strengthens me." Yes, we "overwhelmingly conquer through Him who loved us" (Romans 8:37). Jesus revealed His command of heavenly armies when He asked, "Do you think that I cannot appeal to My Father, and He will at once put at My disposal more than twelve legions of angels?" (Matthew 26:53). We know that one day heaven will open and Jesus will return, seated on a white horse, and in righteousness He will judge and wage war. He is called Faithful and True, and followed by the armies of heaven, He will strike down the nations (Revelation 19:11-15).

DECLARE YAHWEH SABAOTH

When you face giants in your life, whether a weakness, an affliction, or a person, run to Yahweh Sabaoth, the Ruler and Commander of the armies of heaven, and watch what He will accomplish in your life. Pray to Him, *Yahweh Sabaoth, You alone are the one in charge of all things and have at Your disposal all resources, all the armies of heaven. Send help to me today. You are the God of deliverances, able to deliver me in and through and even out of my circumstance. Help me today, Lord, in the way that only You can as Lord of hosts.* Then, say to your mind, heart, and soul, *Nothing I face today is greater than Yahweh Sabaoth, the Lord of hosts. Like David, I am unmoved by the enemy who would dare to taunt the living God, who is my Yahweh Sabaoth, the Lord of hosts. He is able to fight the battle I face today and is stronger than any enemy. His strength is enough to help me through today, tomorrow, and forever. Indeed, I can, as Paul says in Philippians 4:13, do all things through Christ who strengthens me. And I must always remember that my cries reach the ears of the Lord of Sabaoth, as promised in James 5:4.*

Finally, what do you say to the world about Yahweh Sabaoth? Paul encourages you to be wise, to make the most of the opportunity, and to season your speech with grace (Colossians 4:6). Remain unmoved by the taunts of the enemy, who would even wage war in your heart with words that would tempt you to fear, panic, live in a state of anxiety, and finally flee before your enemies. Instead, be strong in the Lord and in the strength of His might (Ephesians 6:10). Imagine yourself as a David coming up against the giant, or even the king, who presumed to say that he was only a boy. Say, "The Lord is my refuge and strength, my very present help in times of trouble, my deliverer, and I come in the name of the Lord of hosts" (see 1 Samuel 17:37,45; Psalm 46:1).

DEPEND ON YAHWEH SABAOTH

Trusting in Yahweh Sabaoth means running to Him in your difficulty and asking Him for help and deliverance. This is especially true when your challenge is more than a match for your capacity to endure and your burden is greater than your strength. A traveler to South America describes a conflict he witnessed between a small animal and a large poisonous snake. The little creature was clearly no match for the vicious serpent. The small animal fearlessly faced its antagonist but was severely wounded by a strike from the poisonous fangs of the snake. The small creature, licking its wounds, ran into the forest to the sustaining plantain tree and hungrily devoured some of its leaves for strength. After some time, the little animal turned around seemingly refreshed and restored, and ran back to resume battle with the snake. This process occurred again and again until finally, from exhaustion, the huge snake lay dead.

Friend, will you run to the Lord of hosts today, who commands all the armies of heaven to come to your aid? He is, as Psalm 68:20 declares, a God of deliverances. I love the plural form—*deliverances*—signifying there are many kinds of deliverances. Sometimes God will deliver you out of a trouble, and sometimes He will deliver you through the trouble. This was the case with Moses in the wilderness for 40 years with a grumbling, idolatrous people, when God gave Moses the strength to endure. You may not seem like much to those around you, but when you know Yahweh Sabaoth, you can be like David, a young boy, ready to fight giants in the name of His Lord. Shout confidently with David, "But we will trust in the name of the LORD, our God" (Psalm 20:7 NIV).

DELIGHT IN YAHWEH SABAOTH

My way is dark, the billows groan,
No guiding star I see;
My storm-tossed ship sails on alone
Upon life's bounding sea.

I cannot guide it anymore
No matter how I try;
But we together, shall reach shore—
My precious Lord and I.
Fear and weakness make me low,
I change with night and dawn.
One day I feel my courage grow,
The next day it is gone;
But never does He change like me
Though angry waves toss high;
I fail, but still we sail the sea—
My precious Lord and I.
He knows where every danger lies,
He sails on through the squall;
He has no fear of sea or skies
Because He made them all.
But some sweet day He'll still the foam
As heaven's shores draw nigh;
We'll anchor in the Port of Home—
My precious Lord and I.[2]

DONALD L. WALKER

My Response

DATE:

KEY VERSE: "You come to me with a sword, a spear, and a javelin, but I come to you in the name of the LORD of hosts, the God of the armies of Israel, whom you have taunted" (1 Samuel 17:45).

FOR FURTHER THOUGHT: What giant is rearing its ugly head today and screaming taunts at you, perhaps trying to tell you it's all over, to give up, that there is no hope? Run to Yahweh Sabaoth, confident He will deliver you through or out of your difficulty. You can hope in Him regardless of what the enemy says. Write a prayer to Yahweh Sabaoth today, asking Him to fight the giants in your life.

MY RESPONSE:

Day Twenty-Seven

TRUSTING IN YAHWEH RO'I—HE IS YOUR SHEPHERD

The LORD is my shepherd,
I shall not want.

PSALM 23:1

Trusting in Yahweh Ro'i gives you assurance that God is always watching over you. Whether you are leading others in ministry, caring for your family, or handling a difficult job, there is one greater than yourself who is taking care of you. His name is Yahweh Ro'i, your Shepherd. David, the shepherd of God's people, knew that he also had a Shepherd. He said, "The LORD is my shepherd, I shall not want" (Psalm 23:1). How can you handle the days when you feel overwhelmed with obstacles or worries? Knowing you have a Shepherd who cares for you, Yahweh Ro'i, will give you confidence to carry out great responsibilities in life.

DISCOVER YAHWEH RO'I

The Hebrew words translated "The LORD is my shepherd" are *Yahweh Ro'i*, first used by David in Psalm 23:1. The word *shepherd* (*ro'eh*) is used at least 80 times throughout the Bible. Following David's reference to the Lord as his Shepherd, God is seen as the Shepherd of His people in Isaiah 40:11, referring to the greatness of God, and in Ezekiel 34:11-16, referring to the restoration of Israel. This new view of God as the Shepherd of His people is typical of the progressive revelation of the character and attributes of God by God Himself. A Hebrew form of the word *shepherd* is also used in reference to God's relationship with Moses in Exodus 33:11, where He spoke (from the pillar of cloud) with Moses face-to-face (at the entrance to the tent of meeting), just as a man speaks to his friend. Jesus refers to Himself as the good shepherd in John 10:11. He is called the great Shepherd (Hebrews 13:20), the Shepherd and Guardian of your souls (1 Peter 2:25), the Chief Shepherd (1 Peter 5:4), and the Lamb who will be "their shepherd, and will guide them to springs of the water of life" (Revelation 7:17).

DRAW NEAR TO YAHWEH RO'I

Yahweh Ro'i is perhaps the most personal and precious name of God ever revealed to His people. How fitting that David, the man after God's own heart, would be given the privilege to present the Lord as our Shepherd. For who could define the beauty or tenderness of the Shepherd better than David, a man who knew the relationship of a shepherd to his sheep, having watched over his own flocks, both in the fields and as king of the people of Israel.

David's explanation of his Shepherd, the Lord, in Psalm 23 has become the most beloved of all psalms and has comforted many a weary traveler on the road of life. Spurgeon called Psalm 23 "the Pearl of Psalms whose soft and pure radiance delights every eye." David reveals to us the benefits of having the Lord as our Shepherd. He meets all of our needs, gives us rest, leads us, restores us, makes us righteous, comforts us even in our last days on earth, stays with us, keeps us from fear, protects us from our enemies, gives us overflowing and abundant life, and ultimately leads us to eternal life.

Many of these benefits David outlines in Psalm 23 are amplified thematically throughout the Bible in both the names of God and the works of God in our lives. Yahweh Ro'i is our Shepherd (verse 1), Yahweh Jireh supplies our needs so we will not be in want (verse 1), Yahweh Shalom gives us peace (seen in the green pastures and quiet waters of verse 2), Yahweh Rophe is our healer (seen in the restoring of our soul in verse 3), Yahweh Tsidkenu is our righteousness (seen in the paths of righteousness of verse 3), Yahweh Nissi is our victory (seen in the table He prepares in the presence of our enemies in verse 5), Yahweh Mekaddesh is the one who sanctifies you (seen in the anointing of our head with oil in verse 5), and Yahweh Shammah is "the Lord who is there" (seen in the presence of the Lord with those who have Him as their Shepherd in verse 4).

Countless other verses testify to the ways God cares for us. God supplies our needs according to His riches in glory in Christ Jesus (Philippians 4:19), gives us rest for our souls (Jeremiah 6:16; Matthew 11:29), leads us in the way we should go (Isaiah 48:17), gives us times of refreshing (Acts 3:19), gives us righteousness through faith in Jesus Christ (Romans 5:17; Philippians 3:9), gives us abundant comfort through Christ (2 Corinthians 1:5), never leaves us or forsakes us (Hebrews 13:5), does not want us to be afraid (Isaiah 41:10), and delivers us from all our fears (Psalm 34:4), gives us armor so we may stand firm against the schemes of the devil (Ephesians 6:11), came to give us abundant life (John 10:10), and gives eternal life to all who believe in His only begotten Son, Jesus Christ (John 3:16).

Trusting in Jesus as the Good Shepherd

"I am the good shepherd, and I know My own and my own know Me" (John 10:14).

In the name *Yahweh Ro'i* we see an intimate relationship between the Shepherd and His sheep. The very name of *Shepherd* reveals to us that we are His sheep. Always remember who you are and whose you are. You are a sheep. And you belong to the Lord your Shepherd. There is one who is always watching over you and caring for you.

Jesus further amplifies this truth when He reveals He is the good shepherd, He knows His sheep, and His sheep know Him (John 10:14).

The sheep follow their Shepherd because they know His voice—they hear Him calling their name (John 10:3-4). Jesus then revealed a powerful truth about the shepherd's heart when He said, "The good shepherd lays down His life for the sheep" (John 10:11). Then he explained, "I lay down My life for the sheep" (John 10:15). The Shepherd loves His sheep so much, with such care and tenderness, that He will lay down His own life to save them. Paul tells us that "God demonstrates His own love toward us, in that while we were yet sinners, Christ died for us" (Romans 5:8).

So draw near and know the heart of your Shepherd, who lays down His life for you, His sheep. Here is what He did for you because of His tender care for you: He bore your griefs, carried your sorrows, and was pierced for your transgressions, crushed for your iniquities, and scourged so you might be healed (Isaiah 53:4-5). He was led like a lamb to the slaughter and crushed, bearing the iniquities of us who, like sheep, have gone astray (Isaiah 53:7-12). Jesus, your Shepherd, is the door to eternal life, where you may enter, be saved, and find pasture (John 10:9).

Nathan Stone pointed out that shepherding in Palestine had not changed much over the years:

> The Palestine shepherd lives night and day with his animals. He establishes a degree of intimacy with them which is touching to observe. He calls them all by their names and they, knowing his voice and hearing his only, heed that voice. He protects the sheep from thieves and preying animals, who would devour them at night, by sleeping in the opening of the often makeshift sheepfold and they, sensing his watchfulness, fear no evil. He provides pasture and water even in the wilderness and the presence of the enemies and they, casting all their anxiety upon him, are fed. There is a singular communion between the shepherd and his sheep.[1]

What does knowing Yahweh Ro'i tell you about yourself? You are a sheep, and you need Him as your Shepherd. Do you, dear friend, know this tender and intimate communion with your Shepherd? Draw near and declare His name, that you might know and trust in Yahweh Ro'i today.

DECLARE YAHWEH RO'I

You need to draw near to Yahweh Ro'i every day of your life, for He is your Shepherd, caring for you, tenderly watching over you, and at times, even carrying you. Draw near to Him and ask for His help, His wisdom, and His care for your every need. Say, *Yahweh Ro'i, thank You that You are my Shepherd. Thank You for promising to search for me, seek me out, care for me, feed me, and deliver me (Ezekiel 34:11-12). Carry me when I cannot walk and lead me when I am unsure of my way. I trust You with my very life.*

Then say to your mind, heart, and soul the words of Psalm 23: "The Lord is my Shepherd, I shall not want...surely goodness and lovingkindness will follow me all the days of my life, and I will dwell in the house of the LORD forever." Finally, tell the world to "seek the LORD while He may be found; call upon Him while He is near" (Isaiah 55:6).

DEPEND ON YAHWEH RO'I

When Jesus speaks of His relationship with His sheep, He points to the intimacy He knows with those who belong to Him. He also reveals how He leads and guides His sheep—His sheep hear His voice calling them by name, and then, in the hearing of His instructions, they follow Him (John 10:1-18). Two questions present themselves to those who are in the church, the body of Christ: Do you know your Shepherd intimately, and do you hear His Word? Clearly, Jesus wants intimacy with you, and He wants you to know His voice and hear what He has to say. This is a wake-up call: "Church, are you intimate with your Shepherd, and are you opening the pages of His Word to hear Him speak?"

My friend Shirley tells the story of her Aunt Sally who ran quickly to the barn as the ewes were giving birth to the lambs. Sally's husband, Ray, put her in charge of the bum lambs, those lambs that were rejected by their mothers, a common occurrence with ewes who had multiple births. Bum lambs were hand raised by the ranchers until they were grown and assimilated into the general flock of sheep. Aunt Sally took the first little lamb, rejected by its mother, cradled him close to her, and rubbed him down with an old towel. She noticed two little humps on its head where horns would eventually grow and whispered softly, "I'll call you Buckaroo."

Just then, her husband opened the door of the kitchen, "I can't understand it," he said. "These ewes are so stubborn—here are two more who need your special care." She picked up one of the little lambs. "You'll be Fluffy," she informed him as she rubbed him down, fluffing up the wool. She gathered up the third little lamb. "With these short little legs," she said, "who could you be but Stumpy!" Just as she finished drying and feeding her three little special lambs, Ray came through the door with one more bum and said, "This is the last one." Aunt Sally washed him, fed him, and called him Lefty because he was the only one left.

For the next few weeks, Aunt Sally cared for her little lambs, calling them each by their names many times a day. She grew attached to them as they played, ate, and slept in the yard of the ranch house. Aunt Sally reluctantly let her lambs join the rest of the sheep to go with the ranch hands to the summer pasture.

One day, at the end of summer, she heard the noise of the sheep coming home. She ran to find her lambs, forgetting how different they would look after three months. When she looked out over all the sheep, she could not distinguish one from another. Then, an idea came to Aunt Sally. She leaned against the fence and began calling her lambs by name. "Fluffy!" "Stumpy!" "Buckaroo!" "Lefty!" Over and over again she called out their names. One by one, three sheep made their way over to the fence. She could clearly distinguish all three. "Why, I know you, you are Buckaroo—those little horns are growing…Here's Fluffy, with all that wool…And this has to be Stumpy!" she exclaimed. "But where's Lefty?" She called again, but it was apparent that Lefty's ears had grown dull to the voice of the shepherdess.

Friends, there's a great lesson in this true story for all of us. Those three sheep knew the voice of their shepherd so well. Do you know your Lord, your good Shepherd, or are you like Lefty, whose ears had grown dull? When you spend time in your Lord's Word, you will grow accustomed to hearing His voice and recognize His call to you. Sadly, there are many in the church whose hearing has grown dull. No wonder Jesus often said, "If anyone has ears to hear, let him hear" (Mark 4:23). In fact, Jesus often spoke in parables because He said the hearts of the people had become dull, their ears could scarcely hear, and they had closed their eyes.

If you haven't yet discovered the excitement of opening the Bible and hearing your Shepherd speak to you, I am calling out to you with the words of Jesus in Revelation 3:2, "Wake up." If you do love His Word and know Him, I encourage you to stay close to your Shepherd. Do not let anything or anyone pull you away from following Him. When you have a need, run to your Shepherd. If you are in trouble, you need your Shepherd. He is with you and promises to never leave or forsake you (Hebrews 13:5). You can count on Him.

DELIGHT IN YAHWEH RO'I

Dorothy Ann Thrupp, born in 1779 in England, wrote many wonderful hymns for the church. One of the very best reveals her obvious love for her Shepherd—"Savior, like a Shepherd Lead Us."

Savior, like a shepherd lead us, much we need Thy tender care;
In Thy pleasant pastures feed us, for our use Thy folds prepare.
Blessed Jesus, blessed Jesus! Thou hast bought us, Thine we are.

We are Thine, Thou dost befriend us, be the guardian of our way;
Keep Thy flock, from sin defend us, seek us when we go astray.
Blessed Jesus, blessed Jesus! Hear, O hear us when we pray.

Thou hast promised to receive us, poor and sinful though we be;
Thou hast mercy to relieve us, grace to cleanse and power to free.
Blessed Jesus, blessed Jesus! We will early turn to Thee.

Early let us seek Thy favor, early let us do Thy will.
Blessed Lord and only Savior, with Thy love our bosoms fill.
Blessed Jesus, blessed Jesus! Thou hast loved us, love us still.

My Response

DATE:

KEY VERSE: "The LORD is my shepherd, I shall not want" (Psalm 23:1).

FOR FURTHER THOUGHT: How do you need Yahweh Ro'i, your Shepherd, today? Do you know Him? Do you love Him? Do you love His Word?

MY RESPONSE:

Day Twenty-Eight

TRUSTING IN ABBA, FATHER—HE IS YOUR FATHER

The Spirit you received does not make you slaves, so that you live in fear again; rather, the Spirit you received brought about your adoption to sonship. And by him we cry, "Abba, Father."

ROMANS 8:15 TNIV

Knowing Abba, Father reveals the privileges of your relationship with God. You are adopted into the family of God because of what Jesus accomplished on the cross for you. Paul tells us that "the Spirit you received does not make you slaves, so that you live in fear again; rather, the Spirit you received brought about your adoption to sonship. And by him we cry, *Abba,* Father" (Romans 8:15 TNIV). The word *adoption,* used by Paul regarding our new relationship with God, signifies "being granted the full rights and privileges of sonship in a family to which one does not belong by nature."[1] You are now granted the privilege of addressing God as your Father with the same words Jesus used to address His Father. This reveals the most tender, precious part of your relationship with God, where you are taken near to the heart of your heavenly Father, who loves you. Do you ever doubt your future, become discouraged with earthly relationships, or question your own significance? You can find hope in the promise that you may run to God and address Him as your Abba, Father.

DISCOVER ABBA, FATHER

We first discover the name *Abba, Father* when Jesus addressed Him with these words in the garden of Gethsemane. He said, "Abba! Father! All things are possible for You; remove this cup from Me; yet not what I will, but what You will" (Mark 14:36). *Abba* is the Aramaic word translated "Father" and is used in the spirit of a tender, affectionate child ("Daddy"). The early church fathers (Chrysostom, Theodore of Mopsuestia, and Theodore of Cyrrhus) who came from Antioch, where Aramaic was spoken, all agreed that *Abba* was the word small children used to approach and address their fathers.[2] The Talmud refers to a weaned child addressing a father with the word *Abba*. In modern Hebrew, it means "Daddy" and is one of the first words a baby learns.

Jesus commonly used *Abba* and *Father* in His prayers and in His references to God (156 times).[3] The use of *Father* (*Pater* in the Greek) to refer to God is rarely seen in the Old Testament, and its common and repeated use to address God and express an intimate relationship with Him is ushered in by Jesus Himself.[4] We see not only that He called His Father with this affectionate name but also that now, thanks to our new relationship with God through Him, we too may use this expression of endearment. Imagine that, in addition to trusting in all the other names of God, we also have the privilege of using the words *Papa, Daddy,* and *Father* in addressing our God. What can that mean except that we have now been ushered into an even more intimate relationship with our God? According to Paul, now that we are adopted to sonship, we may now call Him "*Abba,* Father."

DRAW NEAR TO ABBA, FATHER

Our privilege and authority to call God "Our Father" is seen in the beginning phrase of the Lord's Prayer in Matthew 6:9 (NIV), "Our Father in heaven." Jesus called on His Father with different variations of the name: "My Father who is in heaven" (Matthew 10:32), "Father, Lord of heaven and earth" (Matthew 11:25), "Father" (Matthew 11:26), "My heavenly Father" (Matthew 15:13), "Abba! Father!" (Mark 14:36), "the Father" (John 8:28), and "righteous Father" (John 17:25). Jesus repeatedly calling God "My Father" and thus claiming a unique, intimate relationship with Him as His Son must have been radical for the day considering this was not the common way the Jewish people normally addressed God or even talked about God. He even declared, "I have come in my Father's name" (John 5:43). The New Testament further demonstrates the use of the name *Father* through such titles as "our Father" (Romans 1:7), "the Father" (Romans 6:4), "*Abba,* Father" (Romans 8:15, Galatians 4:6), "the God and Father of our Lord Jesus Christ" (Romans 15:6), "Father of mercies" (2 Corinthians 1:3), "Father of glory" (Ephesians 1:17), "Father of all" (Ephesians 4:6), "God the Father" (1 Thessalonians 1:1), "Father of spirits" (Hebrews 12:9), and "Father of lights" (James 1:17).

Why would I take the time to list all of these different uses of *Father?* We have already seen that God's revelation of Himself to His people is progressive over time. As you can see, *Father* is the name for God written throughout the New Testament (at least 300 times). Because He is your Abba, Father, the one you may call with such an expression of affection, you may be assured of what this name of God says about you—you are His child and part of the family of God. Don't ever forget who you are and whose you are. Because of your adoption as His child, you are granted both the privileges and the responsibilities of the family of God.

You have the privilege of experiencing God's love. John says, "See how great a love the Father has bestowed on us, that we would be called children of God; and such we are" (1 John 3:1). And oh, how great His love is! A.W. Tozer describes it this way:

> Because God is self-existent, His love had no beginning; because He is eternal, His love can have no end; because

He is infinite, it has no limit; because He is holy, it is the quintessence of all spotless purity; because He is immense, His love is an incomprehensibly vast, bottomless, shoreless sea before which we kneel in joyful silence and from which the loftiest eloquence retreats confused and abashed.[5]

You have the privilege of swimming in the ocean of your Father's love.

You now have the privilege of prayer. You may run into the throne room of God as children would run to their fathers or mothers. We may "draw near with confidence to the throne of grace, so that we may receive mercy and find grace to help in time of need" (Hebrews 4:16).

You have the privilege of eternal life. You are going to live forever with your Father in heaven. Eternal life is all wrapped up in Jesus—"God has given us eternal life, and this life is in His Son. He who has the Son has the life; he who does not have the Son of God does not have the life" (1 John 5:11-12).

You have the privilege of receiving an inheritance. Your inheritance is greater than any earthly inheritance you could ever receive. The Father has qualified you to "share in the inheritance of the saints" (Colossians 1:12). Our inheritance comes to us through Christ (Ephesians 1:11) and is a reward (Colossians 3:24).

You have responsibilities too: obedience, holy living, not partaking of the world, and sharing in suffering, all as a result of your new relationship. Peter instructs us, "As obedient children...be holy yourselves also in all your behavior" (1 Peter 1:14-15). God wants us to live holy lives, and so, as our Father, "He disciplines us for our good, so that we may share His holiness" (Hebrews 12:10). As children of God we will suffer as we share in the sufferings of Christ (1 Peter 4:13). As children of our Father, we are not to love the world or the things in the world (1 John 2:15).

One truth stands out above all—we have a future and hope because God is our Father and we are His children. One day we will stand face-to-face with Him and experience the reality of our relationship with God in a completely new way. He says, "I will be their God and they will be my children" (Revelation 21:7 TNIV). What a day it will be to see the throne of God and of the Lamb! There will no longer be any night, no lamps, and no light from the sun because the light of the Lord will brighten up the atmosphere of heaven. We will have the right to the tree of life and will be able to enter the city of God (Revelation 22:14).

Because you are a child of God, you are granted the privilege of calling Him Abba, Father, of running to Him, and of falling into His everlasting arms and whispering *Papa* or *Daddy.* Perhaps you cannot yet grasp what this kind of closeness with your heavenly Father means. You need to understand the Father's heart—He longs for this relationship with you. He wants your company and your communion with Him. He loves having you with Him. He wants to hear everything you say. He desires to take care of you. Remember, He is the one who said to Israel, "I will not forget you. Behold, I have inscribed you on the palms of My hands; Your walls are continually before me" (Isaiah 49:15-16).

I think of the early morning ritual at my brother's house. My little niece, Kayla, runs into the room, crawls into her daddy's lap, with her daddy's arms quickly pulling her close to his heart. Her daddy says, "Kayla, have I told you yet?"

Kayla says, "I know, Daddy."

He responds, "What do you know?"

She says, "You love me."

Then her daddy says, "Kayla, your daddy loves you more than anything. I love you today, tomorrow, and always."

What a picture of Abba, Father's love! No wonder, when Jesus knew He was going to the cross, He fell on the ground in prayer with His Father and cried out the most tender of all names, *Abba, Father. Abba* reveals the most intimate of all father-child relationships. You are now given that same tender, intimate, affectionate, and blessed relationship with your Father.

What does knowing Abba, Father tell you about yourself? You are a child of God. You are a recipient of His great love. Your new privileges with God as your Abba, Father seem almost too good to be true. And yet, the Father has promised it, Jesus has accomplished it, and the indwelling Holy Spirit has guaranteed it. And so, draw near and call out to your Abba, Father.

DECLARE ABBA, FATHER

Dear friend, do not ever forget that you are a child of God. When the world is "too much with you," withdraw from the busyness of life and draw near to your Father. Lay every one of your needs, desires, difficulties—indeed, every request in His able hands. Pray, *Abba, Father, thank You for calling me Your child, forgiving my sins, giving me eternal life, and qualifying me to share in the inheritance of the saints. Such truths are almost more than I can fathom, and yet You promise. Thank You, Father, that what You promise, You will do.* Then say to your mind, heart, and soul, *I am a child of God. My Father has qualified me to share in the inheritance of His people in the kingdom. He has rescued me from the dominion of darkness and brought me into the kingdom of the Son He loves. He has redeemed me and forgiven my sins. This life is but for a brief moment compared to eternity, and I will live with Him forever.*

Finally, say to the world, "Today is the day to make a decision to receive Christ and be a part of the family of God. A day is going to come when the Father makes all things new. He will give to the one who thirsts from the spring of the water of life without cost. He who overcomes will inherit these things, and the Father will be his God, and he will be God's son (Revelation 21:3-7). Today is the day of decision for Christ." And if there is one who responds, desiring to know Christ personally, then pray with them: *Lord Jesus, I need You. Thank You for dying on the cross for my sins. I invite You now to come into my life, forgive my sins, and make me the person You want me to be. In Jesus' name, Amen.*

DEPEND ON ABBA, FATHER

One of my favorite stories growing up was *A Little Princess* by Frances Hodgson Burnett. The story is about a little girl named Sara Crewe, who was entrusted by her affluent father to the care of a boarding school for girls while he went to Africa to serve in the army. One day, word came of the tragic death of Sara's father. Miss Minchin, the greedy headmistress, immediately put the now-penniless Sara to work for her room and board. She moved Sara to a cold, dark attic room and gave her black and gray dingy clothing to wear. Life was very dismal and difficult for Sara.

But then the servant next door noticed Sara through the attic window. He told his master, Mr. Carrisford, of poor Sara's miserable existence. They devised a plan to begin secretly giving her gifts. While she was sleeping and working, the servant and his assistants crossed the roof and brought furniture, rugs, books, and other presents and completely transformed the room, even lighting a fire in the fireplace and leaving a lavish meal and luxurious clothes. No one at the boarding school even knew about the transformation.

In the meantime, Mr. Carmichael, the attorney for Mr. Carrisford, had been trying to find the daughter of Captain Crewe, the lost Sara Crewe, in order to give her the amassed fortune of her father. One evening Mr. Carrisford's pet monkey escaped over to Sara's attic room. When Sara returned the monkey, she shared that she was born in India, and soon her identity was discovered. Her life changed immediately. With her fortune restored, she moved out of the boarding school and became the charge of her new guardian, Mr. Carrisford.

I have always loved this story because it helps me visualize the new relationship I have with my Father in heaven. The transformation of Sara's room and life reminds me of the amazing transformation my Father has made in my own life. He has given me everything—an eternal inheritance, a new life, complete forgiveness, the privilege of talking with Him anytime, power and strength to live through the Holy Spirit, and so much more.

What is the greatest sign of trust in your heavenly Father? It's living as a child of your Father. Look at Jesus to learn how to live with your Father. Notice that He would often withdraw to a quiet place to talk with His Father (Luke 5:16). He was obedient to the Father. His great desire was to do the will of the Father and accomplish His work. He always thanked His Father. He prayed to the Father about His ministry and His disciples. And in His darkest hour, in the garden of Gethsemane, He cried out to His Father, "*Abba!* Father!"

Some of us carry tremendous burdens of responsibility or heavy loads of suffering. And perhaps you are feeling as though the weight of the world is on your shoulders. Depending on God means you must assume the position the name *Abba, Father* reveals to you—you are a child. But you are not just any child. You are a child of the one who is Elohim, El Elyon, El

Shaddai, El Roi, Adonai, Yahweh, Yahweh Jireh, Yahweh Sabaoth, Yahweh Mekaddesh. This same God you have drawn near to through many different names on this 30-day journey is also your Abba, Father. First and foremost, you are a child of the King.

DELIGHT IN ABBA, FATHER

The greatest words you can say in praise to your Father are the words that Jesus said to His Father: "O righteous Father, although the world has not known You, yet I have known You" (John 17:25).

DATE:

KEY VERSE: "The Spirit you received does not make you slaves, so that you live in fear again; rather, the Spirit you received brought about your adoption to sonship. And by him we cry, '*Abba,* Father'" (Romans 8:15 TNIV).

FOR FURTHER THOUGHT: What is most significant to you about the name *Abba, Father*? How do you need your Father today?

MY RESPONSE:

Day Twenty-Nine

TO GOD BE
THE GLORY

*This is eternal life, that they may know
You, the only true God, and Jesus Christ
whom You have sent. I glorified You
on the earth, having accomplished the
work which You have given Me to do.*

JOHN 17:3-4

I have read many classic Christian books, and I feel as if many of the authors have become my friends. Do you know what stands out to me? Most of these men and women are now face-to-face with God. They are not on earth anymore. And yet their lives still speak (Hebrews 11:4). How can a life say something substantial to the world about God? By trusting in the names of God. Trusting His names requires knowing His names.

Knowing God sets all these men and women authors apart from the world. They breathed a rarified air and lived their lives on a higher plane than the average person. They thought great thoughts about God. They reasoned and wrestled with what they read in the Bible until they understood, as best they could, what God was saying to them. And they finished their race well. They were able to say, along with Jesus, "This is eternal life, that they may know You, the only true God, and Jesus Christ whom You have sent. I glorified You on the earth, having accomplished the work which You have given Me to do" (John 17:3-4).

I think of Charles Spurgeon, who wrote more books and articles and sermons in a year than most men or women have written in a lifetime. He inspires me to write and speak more than I think is humanly possible. Then I think of Amy Carmichael, bedridden for the last 20 years of her life, and I am inspired to faithfully love and serve the Lord in the face of the obstacles in my life that sometimes seem to thwart my ability to continue on. I think of Hannah Whitall Smith, who discovered the secret of walking by faith, and I am inspired to live by faith in God's Word even during those times when others seem to be consumed with the things of the world.

I think of my seminary professors Dr. Ronald Youngblood and Dr. Walter Wessel and of their faithful commitment to studying and teaching the Word of God, and I am inspired to live in God's Word and love the Bible even when so very few in the church seem to share that commitment. I think of D.L. Moody, who aimed in life to be the one who was wholeheartedly yielded to God, and I am inspired to live my life fully surrendered to the Lord. I think of Bill and Vonette Bright, who took an idea from God, entrusted that idea to Him, and saw God develop Campus Crusade for Christ, and I am inspired to trust God for the development of Quiet Time Ministries.

I think of Josh and Dottie McDowell, who tirelessly continue to serve the Lord, and I am inspired to serve the Lord day after day even though I watch many in the world carelessly wasting their lives. I think of Henrietta Mears, who told others to dream big because anything less is too small for our great God, and I am inspired to believe God to do immeasurably more than anything I can ask or imagine. All these lives have spoken to me and are still speaking as I run the race the Lord has set before me.

Dear friend, we must step out of the crowd and be counted with those who have joined the company of men and women who have known and trusted and loved God. Many have run their race and have finished well. I say to you with all my heart that I long for you to be one of those great men and women of God who will live in such a way that your life speaks for Him. God is not looking for those who will be famous but for those who will be faithful and finish well. So often we think, *If only I could get rid of the difficulty this situation or that person is causing me, then I could run my race.* But friend, those very things *are* your race. Those very challenges bring opportunities to trust in the names of God, and as a result, to have a life that shouts His names to the world.

When I awaken early in the morning and sit in the family room for my quiet time with the Lord, it is dark outside. No light. But then, within an hour, the sun begins to rise, there is light on the horizon, and I can just make out some of the trees in my backyard. Then, as more time passes, brilliant colors begin to light the sky, and I can see more of my surroundings.

Friend, life is like that. In the darkness of the night, you cannot see anything. But you know the sun is on its way, and the sunrise is right around the corner. And with the dawning of the day, the light brightens the world around you. In the darkness of your trials, you can know that God is still there, and in His time, the heaviness of your difficult night will lift, and the light from His Word can brighten your world and reveal the horizon of your circumstances. It is always too soon to give up. Trusting in the names of God as you discover His name, draw near to His name, declare His name, depend on His name, and delight in His name will bring brilliant color to your day and speak volumes to the world about God. You will declare His glory to others as you shine like a light for Him.

Someday, you are going to step from time into eternity, and you will be face-to-face with your Lord. May His face be so precious to you now that when you look into His eyes then, a familiar, knowing exchange of love will occur between you and Him, a reminder of all the wonderful hours you spent together this side of heaven. Think of that moment when you see Him, and all earthly fears and doubts melt away.

Do not be afraid to dream big and believe God for great and mighty things, for Your God is able to do immeasurably more than all you ask or imagine, according to His power that is at work in you. Join that great company who no longer live for themselves but for Him who died and rose again on their behalf. Be faithful, dear friend, lift your eyes to heaven, bask in the unseen and eternal truths of God in His Word, run your race with endurance, and cross the finish line with your arms held high, shouting the words, "To God be the glory!" Wait until you see His face. Then you will know, dear friend, it was worth it all.

My Response

DATE:

KEY VERSE: "This is eternal life, that they may know You, the only true God, and Jesus Christ whom You have sent. I glorified You on the earth, having accomplished the work which You have given Me to do" (John 17:3-4).

FOR FURTHER THOUGHT: Think about the race the Lord has set before you today. What will it take for you to run your race and finish well? What does seeing the Lord's face when you step from time into eternity mean to you? Close your time today by writing a prayer, expressing all that is on your heart.

MY RESPONSE:

QUIET TIME WEEK FIVE: TRUSTING GOD AS DAVID DID

*God sees not as man sees, for man
looks at the outward appearance,
but the LORD looks at the heart.*

1 Samuel 16:7

PREPARE YOUR HEART

You have spent the last 29 days discovering the names of God and the great value of trusting in His names. The Bible speaks of heroes who trusted in God, and when they did, God did extraordinary things that only He could do. You have seen some of God's great heroes, such as Abraham, Moses, Hannah, Gideon, and David. One of the greatest lovers of God's names was David. God called David a "man after My heart" (Acts 13:22). David loved the presence of the Lord so much that he wanted to live in His presence and behold His beauty. He must have spent a lot of time with God, for he knew many of His names. Ask the Lord to give you insight into the heart of David, a lover of God who truly knew how to trust in His names.

READ AND STUDY GOD'S WORD

1. The first king of God's people was Saul. But God regretted that He had made Saul king because Saul turned away from following God and did not carry out His commands (1 Samuel 15:10). So God instructed Samuel to go to the family of Jesse, where he would find God's choice for king of His people. Read 1 Samuel 16:1-13 and write out everything you learn about David, the man after God's own heart.

2. While his brothers fought in Saul's army, David was in charge of tending his father's flock of sheep in Bethlehem and carrying provisions to his brothers. Probably no event in the life of David reveals more clearly his knowledge of the names of God than the battle with Goliath. Read 1 Samuel 17:17-54 and write down your most significant insights about the character of David.

3. Look at the following verses from the psalms of David and write everything you learn about the names of God.

Psalm 22:22

Psalm 23:3

Psalm 29:2

Psalm 30:4

Psalm 31:3

Psalm 34:3

Psalm 143:11

4. Describe how important the names of God were to David.

ADORE GOD IN PRAYER

Think back over the past 30 days and all you have learned about the names of God. Ask the Lord to apply what you have learned to your life in such a meaningful way that you will, day by day, trust in the names of God.

YIELD YOURSELF TO GOD

Meditate on the following words by Alan Redpath:

> You may not be intellectual or well thought of in your family circle; you may be despised by others for your faith in Christ. Perhaps you had only a little share in the love of your parents, as David did. But remember that those who are rejected of men often become beloved of the Lord. Your faith in the Lord Jesus may be very weak and you may realize little of the dignity which Christ has purposed for you, but the thought of God toward you began before He ever flung a star into space. Then He wrote your name on His heart; it was graven in the palm of His hand before the sky was stretched out in the heavens. You may consider yourself very obscure and unknown, just a unit in the mass, a cog in the machine. Like David, you might well say, "I was a beast before thee" (Psalm 73:22), and

"I am a worm, and no man" (Psalm 22:6). Yet in His abundant mercy God can stoop down from heaven's highest glory to lift a beggar from the dunghill and set him among princes.[1]

ENJOY HIS PRESENCE

Turn back to day 1 and read what you wrote in your letter to the Lord. As you think about this 30-day journey, summarize in a few sentences the most important truths you have learned. What was your favorite day of reading and why? Also, what is your favorite name of God? How will this journey make a difference in your life, and what will you carry with you?

REST IN HIS LOVE

"May the name of the God of Jacob set you securely on high…May He grant you your heart's desire and fulfill all your counsel! We will sing for joy over your victory. And in the name of our God we will set up our banners…Some boast in chariots and some in horses, but we will boast in the name of the LORD, our God" (Psalm 20:1-7).

Notes—Week Five

APPENDIXES

DISCUSSION QUESTIONS

These questions are for people who share this 30-day journey together. This book is a great tool for helping you talk together about how to know and trust God. It also provides for a great 30-day preparation for one of the books of quiet times available from Quiet Time Ministries. God bless you as you help others discover the magnificent character and attributes of God.

Introduction

Use the introduction week to meet those in your group, hand out copies of this book, familiarize everyone with the topic of knowing and trusting in God and His names, and play the introduction message (if you are using the weekly DVD messages for *Trusting in the Names of God*). Begin your group time by asking, "What brought you to this 30-day journey? How did you hear about it?" Allow everyone to share. Then pass out the books and show those in your group how each week is organized, with a quiet time as the sixth day. Show your group all the information in appendix 2. Make certain they know about the names of God worksheet in case they would like to write out each name of God they discover on the journey. Tell your group about the websites www.trustinginthenamesofgod.com, www.quiettime.org, and www.myquiettime.com as well as the Quiet Time Café message board at www.quiettimecafe.com, where they may share insights online with others. Then describe how you will structure each week's meeting. You may want to use a signup sheet for snacks. Close in prayer.

Week One: Knowing God's Names

DAY 1: The Great Adventure of Knowing God

1. Begin your time together in prayer. You may want to open your time of discussion by reading *A Prayer of Trust* by A.W. Tozer on the page just before the introduction.

2. As you lead your group through a discussion of each day, you may want to have someone read the verse at the beginning of each day. Then, as you begin this discussion, ask your group to share what it meant to them to spend daily time this last week thinking about the names of God.

3. How did the introduction encourage you and prepare you for this 30-day journey? Why are you excited about studying the names of God? What was your favorite phrase in "The Thought of God" by Frederick William Faber?

4. Day 1 begins with the statement, "The greatest claim you can make in your life is that you know God." What do you think about that statement and why?

5. Why is knowing God a great adventure? How has He surprised you in your relationship with Him?

6. What has been the most important truth you have learned about God this week?

7. What was your favorite statement in day 1 about the great adventure of knowing God? What challenged you? What encouraged you?

DAY 2: God Has Revealed Himself to You

1. In day 2 you learned that God has revealed Himself. Why is that important, and what does it mean to you?

2. In what ways has God revealed Himself?

3. What have you learned about God from His revelation of Himself?

4. If you prayed a prayer to receive Christ for the first time, you can know that the Lord Jesus lives in you and that you have now begun the great adventure of knowing God.

DAY 3: You Can Know His Names

1. Why is knowing the names of God important if you want to know God better?

2. In what way is God issuing an invitation to us when He gives us His names?

3. What was your favorite quote from day 3?

DAY 4: Responding to the Names of God

1. How does knowing God's names change our lives?

2. Describe what it means to calculate the names of God into our lives.

3. Can you think of a time in your own life when knowing who God is, what He does, and what He says has made a difference in your life?

4. What quote or truth encouraged you the most in today's reading?

DAY 5: How to Trust in the Names of God

1. What did you learn about trust in day 5?

2. Why is the acrostic Total Reliance Under Stress and Trial a good description and definition of trust?

3. What was your favorite quote or truth from today's reading?

DAY 6: Knowing God's Names Quiet Time

1. On day 6 you had the opportunity to enjoy a quiet time about knowing God's names. What meant the most to you from the examples of King Hezekiah and King Asa?

2. What was your favorite verse about the names of God?

3. What quote, verse, or insight encouraged you the most this week?

Week Two: Trusting in God's Names

DAY 7: Discover His Names

1. Quickly review what you discussed last week. This will be of special benefit to those who are just joining your group. You might review by sharing what it means to know God, the importance of God's names, and how God has revealed Himself to us. As you lead your group through a discussion of each day in week 2, you may want to have someone read the verse at the beginning of each day.

2. In day 7 we began looking at how to trust in the names of God using this plan: Discover His names, draw near to His names, declare His names, depend on His names, and delight in His names. Review the "Trusting in the Names of God" page for the *Quiet Time Notebook* and "How to Trust in the Names of God" in appendix 2.

3. In day 7, you read the following: "When we ask God to tell us His name, we ask to know Him as He really is." Why is it important to know God as He really is?

4. What kinds of idols are present in our culture today?

5. What are some good ways to discover God's names, character, and attributes?

6. Describe how to discover the names of God. What might you record once you make a discovery?

DAY 8: Draw Near to His Names

1. On day 8 you learned how to draw near to God's names. What are ways you can dig deeper and draw near to God's names?

2. What is the value of slowing down? How are you doing in the art of slowing down?

3. What was your favorite example or quote from today's reading?

DAY 9: Declare His Names

1. In day 9 you learned about declaring God's names. What does it mean to declare His names?

2. What is the value in declaring God's names?

3. What was your favorite quote or example from day 9?

DAY 10: Depend on His Names

1. In day 10 you looked at depending on the names of God. Why is dependence on God's names so important?

2. What will dependence on God require in your life?

3. What was the most important truth you learned from day 10?

4. What was your favorite example in day 10?

5. Describe how you can use what you've learned about God's names to help you trust and depend on Him.

DAY 11: Delight in His Names

1. In day 11 you considered delighting in the names of God. What does it mean to delight in His names?

2. Why is worship and praise the natural result of trusting in the names of God?

3. List some ways you can delight in His names.

4. How can a life that praises and worships God make a difference in the lives of others?

DAY 12: Trusting in God's Names Quiet Time

1. In your quiet time this week on day 12, what did you learn from the example of King Asa?

2. What did you learn from the verses on trust?

3. How do you need to take courage in the Lord in your own life?

4. What was your favorite insight, quote, or verse from your reading and study this week? What have you thought about most this week as you have engaged in this 30-day journey of trusting in the names of God?

Week Three: Discovering God's Greatness and Glory

DAY 13: Trusting in Elohim—He Is Your Creator

1. In the last two weeks we have been talking about the great value of knowing and trusting in the names of God. We have seen that when God gives us His name, He gives us more than just a designation. He tells us who He is, and we gain insight into His personality and character. Last week we talked about how to trust in the names of God by discovering His names, drawing near to His names, declaring His names, depending on His names, and delighting in His names. What is the most important thing you've learned so far in this 30-day journey of trusting in the names of God? (As you lead your group through a discussion of each day in week 3, you may want to have someone read the verse at the beginning of each day.)

2. In day 13 we began looking at names of God. The first name you read about was *Elohim*. When God gives us the name *Elohim*, what is He revealing about Himself?

3. What difference does knowing Elohim make in your life?

4. What was your favorite truth about Elohim?

5. What was your favorite quote?

DAY 14: Trusting in El Elyon—He Is Your Sovereign

1. In day 14 we looked at the name *El Elyon*. What does this name mean?

2. Describe the situation in which God introduced the name *El Elyon*.

3. What does the phrase *God is sovereign* mean?

4. How do you see the sovereignty of God at work in the life of Joseph?

5. How have you seen God's sovereignty at work in your own life?

6. What was your favorite quote or illustration in day 14?

DAY 15: Trusting in Adonai—He Is Your Lord

1. In day 15, you looked at the name *Adonai*. What does this name mean?

2. What was the occasion of the revelation of the name *Adonai*?

3. What did you learn about the master-servant relationship?

4. How is Jesus an example for you in serving Adonai?

5. How should we respond to Adonai?

6. How has God brought you to a commitment of serving Him in your own life over the past few years?

DAY 16: Trusting in El Shaddai—He Is Enough for You

1. Who is El Shaddai, and what were the circumstances surrounding the revelation this name?

2. What truths about God do you think about when you hear the name *El Shaddai*?

3. Why is knowing El Shaddai is all-sufficient such a comfort?

4. In what way do you need El Shaddai today?

5. What is the most important truth you learned in day 16?

DAY 17: Trusting in Yahweh Jireh—He Is Your Provider

1. In day 17 you learned about Yahweh Jireh. Describe the circumstances surrounding the use of this name.

2. How did Yahweh Jireh provide for Abraham?

3. Describe the value of tests in life.

4. How have you experienced a test of faith in your own life?

5. How do tests measure the depth of your commitment to the Lord?

6. Can you think of a time when Yahweh Jireh provided for you?

DAY 18: Trusting God As Abraham Did Quiet Time

1. In day 18, you spent time with the Lord, looking at Abraham. What did you notice about Abraham's relationship with the Lord?

2. What was your favorite quote or insight from your quiet time?

3. What was the most important idea or truth you learned from the names of God this week?

4. What was your favorite name of God this week?

Week Four: Discovering God's Person and Presence

DAY 19: Trusting in El Roi—He Sees You

1. It's hard to believe we've already been studying the names of God for four weeks! This week we looked at five more names of God. (As you lead your group through a discussion of each day in week 4, you may want to have someone read the verse at the beginning of each day.)

   As you spent this week thinking about who God is, what was the most important thing you learned? How did God speak to you this week?

2. What did you learn about El Roi, and what was the occasion of this new name for God?

3. How does knowing that El Roi sees you encourage you?

DAY 20: Trusting in Yahweh—He Is Everything You Need

1. Why is *Yahweh* such an important name of God?

2. How did God reveal this name for Himself—what was the

historical situation, and to whom did He reveal Himself as *Yahweh*?

3. Describe the relationship God had with Moses.

4. What did you learn about Yahweh?

5. How did Jesus reveal Yahweh?

6. Can you remember when you realized that the Lord wanted you to know Him and be in an intimate relationship with Him? If so, can you share it with the group?

7. How does knowing Yahweh impact your life? What is your own response to knowing this great name of God? What is it about knowing He is Yahweh that encourages your trust in Him?

DAY 21: Trusting in Yahweh Rophe—He Is Your Healer

1. In day 21 you looked at the name *Yahweh Rophe*. Who is Yahweh Rophe, and what were the circumstances surrounding this name of God?

2. In what ways do we need Yahweh Rophe in our own lives?

3. What was your favorite quote in day 21?

DAY 22: Trusting in Yahweh Nissi—He Is Your Victory

1. Day 22 begins with this statement: "Trusting in Yahweh Nissi gives you confidence in every struggle." Why does trusting in Him bring confidence?

2. Describe the circumstances surrounding the revelation of the name *Yahweh Nissi*.

3. What was the significance of a banner in a battle?

4. In what ways do we experience battles in our own lives?

5. How can Yahweh Nissi help us in our battles?

DAY 23: Trusting in Yahweh Mekaddesh—He Makes You Holy

1. In day 23 you learned about Yahweh Mekaddesh. How did God reveal this name?

2. What is the significance of the name *Yahweh Mekaddesh*, and why does God want us to know this name for Himself?

3. Why is living a holy life so important?

4. What did you read in day 23 that encourages you in the way you live your life?

5. What was your favorite quote?

DAY 24: Trusting God As Moses Did Quiet Time

1. Describe Moses' relationship with God.

2. How does his relationship with God encourage you in your own relationship with the Lord?

3. What was the most important truth you learned from your quiet time?

4. Was there a favorite verse, quote, or insight from the entire week that you would like to share?

Week Five: Discovering God's Care and Concern

DAY 25: Trusting in Yahweh Shalom—He Is Your Peace

1. We have had such an incredible journey together onto such sacred ground, looking at the magnificence of our great God and what it means to trust in Him.

   As you have now finished reading the book, what is the most important thing you've learned as a result of the journey? How will this book and its emphasis on the names of God make a difference in your life? How has it changed your view of your own relationship with the Lord?

2. In day 25 you looked at the name *Yahweh Shalom*. What were the circumstances surrounding the revelation of this name?

3. How did Gideon wrongly interpret God, and what do we sometimes misunderstand about God when we consider our own circumstances?

4. How will trusting in Yahweh Shalom help us in our own lives?

5. What is the value of peace?

DAY 26: Trusting in Yahweh Sabaoth—He Is Your Deliverer

1. In day 26 we looked at the name *Yahweh Sabaoth*. What does that name mean, and what were the circumstances in David's life surrounding that name? How did David experience the work of Yahweh Sabaoth?

2. What are some of the giants we face in life?

3. Have you been able to stand strong against a giant because of Yahweh Sabaoth and His deliverance? Describe your experience.

4. How do you need Yahweh Sabaoth today?

DAY 27: Trusting in Yahweh Ro'i—He Is Your Shepherd

1. In day 27, you looked at the name *Yahweh Ro'i*. Why might the Lord want you to know He is Yahweh Ro'i?

2. How did David know the Lord as his Shepherd?

3. What are the benefits of having a shepherd?

4. What is the most important truth you learned today about Yahweh Ro'i?

5. In what way do you need the Lord as your Shepherd today?

DAY 28: Trusting in Abba, Father—He Is Your Father

1. Day 28 took you into the New Testament to look at another name of God: *Abba, Father*. Who used this name for God, and what does *Abba, Father* mean?

2. What is the significance of the name *Abba, Father*? Why would the Lord want us to know this name?

3. What are the privileges that we now have as a part of the family of God?

4. What is your favorite truth, quote, or illustration from day 28?

DAY 29: To God Be the Glory

1. Read the words of Jesus in John 17:3-4 to your group. Then share the importance of having a life that still speaks. Ask your group whose lives have spoken to them over the years—it may be authors, speakers, teachers, a pastor.

2. How can we run our race well and finish well?

DAY 30: Trusting God As David Did Quiet Time

1. How is David an example for you? What have you learned from his life that will help you in your own relationship with the Lord?

2. As you think about your journey over the last 30 days, what has been most significant to you?

3. What was your favorite name of God?

4. When you read the letter to the Lord you wrote on day 1, how did it help you understand what God has been teaching you?

5. What was your favorite example, verse, or quote in this 30-day journey?

6. Would you like to share anything else as a result of your 30-day journey?

Close in prayer.

Appendix 2

MORE TOOLS FOR TRUSTING IN THE NAMES OF GOD

In this 30-day journey, you have only begun to explore the many wonderful names of God found in the Bible. Below is a selected list of names and attributes for further study in your quiet time. You may choose to meditate on one, looking up the verses and writing your insights in your journal or the *Quiet Time Notebook*. Study these names and attributes further using commentaries, dictionaries, encyclopedias, and word study tools. Enhance your quiet time with the companion devotional Bible study, *Trusting in the Names of God—A Quiet Time Experience*.

NAMES OF GOD

El Gibbor—the Mighty God (Isaiah 9:6)
El Elohe Israel—God, the God of Israel (Genesis 33:20)
El Olam—the Everlasting God (Genesis 21:33)
El Hay—the Living God (Joshua 3:10)
Yahweh Elohay—the Lord My God (Zechariah 14:5)

El Gemuloth—the God of Recompenses (Jeremiah 51:56)

Yahweh Osenu—the Lord Our Maker (Psalm 95:6)

Yahweh Tsuri—the Lord My Rock (Psalm 19:14)

Yahweh Shammah—the Lord Is There (Ezekiel 48:35)

Yahweh Tsidkenu—the Lord Our Righteousness (Jeremiah 23:6)

Yahweh Mishgabbi—the Lord My Fortress (Psalm 18:2)

Yahweh Mephalti—the Lord My Deliverer (Psalm 18:2)

Yahweh Machsi—the Lord My Refuge (Psalm 91:9)

Yahweh Magen—the Lord the Shield (Deuteronomy 33:29)

CHARACTER AND ATTRIBUTES OF GOD

All-Wise: Romans 16:27

Compassionate: Exodus 34:6

Eternal: Psalm 90:1-2

Faithful: Lamentations 3:23

Good: Psalm 100:5

Gracious: Pslam 86:15

Holy: Leviticus 11:44-45

Immutable: James 1:17

Just: Isaiah 30:18

Loving: 1 John 4:7-8

Merciful: Psalm 86:15

Omnipresent: Psalm 139:7-12

Omniscient: Psalm 147:4-5

Righteous: Deuteronomy 11:7

Self-Existent: John 5:26

Self-Sufficient: Acts 17:24-25

Sovereign: 1 Chronicles 29:10-14

Transcendent: Psalm 97:9

Triune: Matthew 28:19

Names of God Observation Study

The name of the LORD is a strong tower;
the righteous runs into it and is safe.
Proverbs 18:10

Scripture Passage _____Psalm 46_____ Date ___10/25/07___

As you read the selected passage, write out everything you learn about who God is, what God does, and what God says. Personalize your observations.

Who God Is

my refuge and strength v. 1
a present help in my trouble v. 1
the LORD of hosts vv. 7, 11 (name of God)
the God of Jacob vv. 7, 11 (name of God)
my stronghold vv. 7, 11

What God Does

in midst of His city v. 5
helps when the morning dawns v. 5
can melt the earth with His voice v. 6
He is with me vv. 7, 11
can make earth desolate, wars to cease, break weapons, burn chariots v. 9

What God Says

Cease striving and know that I am God v. 10
I will be exalted among the nations and earth v. 10

Summary and conclusions:
God is my refuge, my strength, my helper, and my stronghold. He is with me, is powerful, and desires I stop striving and draw near to know Him.

Application in my life:
Lord, I see today that no matter how turbulent my circumstances, You are greater. Thank You for being with me and helping me.

Trusting in the Names of God

Those who know Your name will put their trust in You.
Psalm 9:10

Discover His Name

Name or attribute of God: *God*

Hebrew or Greek transliteration: *Elohim, elohiym*

Significant verse(s): *Genesis 1:1*

Historical context: *Creation*

Strong's number(s): *430*

Definition and description of name or attribute of God: *the true God, masculine plural form, occurs 2600 times in the OT, conveys in Scripture that God is Creator, King, Judge, Lord, and Savior. He is faithful, gracious, and compassionate.*

Draw Near to His Name

Digging deeper—significant verses, reference tools, including commentaries, dictionaries, encyclopedias, books on names and character of God:

Genesis 5:1; Deuteronomy 4:31; 7:9; Psalm 47:7-8; 50:6; 86:12; 116:5; Hosea 13:4

UBS Handbook: Only word for "God" found in the story of creation.

Lockyer: Plurality in unity, occurs 35 times in the first 2 chapters of Genesis, mostly in connection with God's creative power. Used most often in Deuteronomy and Psalms.

Nathan Stone: Expresses general idea of greatness and glory.

William MacDonald: Elohim is self-existent and uncreated.

Trusting in the Names of God

Those who know Your name will put their trust in You.

Psalm 9:10

Declare His Name

LORD, YOU ARE...

my creator and the Triune God. You created all things, the earth, the universe, and even me. You are the Triune God: the Father, the Son, and the Holy Spirit.

Depend on His Name

LORD, I NEED YOU BECAUSE...

of a current impossible situation. Elohim, You are Creator, and You can do anything. You can breathe life into this difficulty. I lay it before You now and I ask You to work out something only You can do.

Delight in His Name

LORD, I LOVE YOU BECAUSE...

You are majestic, eternal, all-powerful, and greater than anything I face today. I love You because You created me, my incredible family, and my friends. You are the Master Designer, who did the most amazing design of the universe and the human body. I love how You chose green for trees and blue for sky. You are perfection and infinite beauty.

How to Trust in the Names of God

1. *Discover His Name*

Look for a name, character, or attribute of God from your Bible reading plan, *Nave's Topical Bible,* a Bible dictionary, a Bible encyclopedia, or books on the names, character, or attributes of God, and/or Bible studies. Write out the name, related verse(s), Hebrew/Greek transliteration, Strong's number(s), and the definition and/or description of the name, character, or attribute.

2. *Draw Near to His Name*

Dig deeper into the meaning of the name, character, or attribute of God through related verses, cross-references, and reference tools including commentaries, dictionaries, encyclopedias, and/or books on the names and character of God.

3. *Declare His Name*

Affirm what you have learned to God Himself, beginning with the words, *Lord, You are...* Then personalize the truths and declare them to your own mind, heart, and soul. Finally, be prepared to tell the world what you have learned and know to be true about God with your life and words.

4. *Depend on His Name*

Apply what you have learned about God to your own life. Your dependence on God will often include a yielding and surrendering of your own desires and plans to say yes to God. Call out to God by praying, *Lord, I need You because...*

5. *Delight in His Name*

Praise and worship God in light of what you have learned about Him. Begin by praying, *Lord, I love You because...*

TRUSTING IN THE NAMES OF GOD WORKSHEET

As you study God's names day by day in this book, write out each Hebrew transliteration. Then write the English word in the Bible for God's name, the meaning, and related Scripture references. See example below for *Elohim*. (This information is also available on a bookmark from our website, www.quiettime. org.)

Hebrew Name	English Name	Meaning	Scripture
Elohim	God	one true God	Genesis 1:1
		mighty one	
		He is Creator	

YAHWEH (YHWH)

Meditate on the person and works of Yahweh:

He will intervene in situations that are oppressive for His people. He is intimately involved in the human struggle and will save and deliver (Exodus 3:7-9; Psalm 34:19).

He is present, accessible, and dynamically near to all who call on Him for forgiveness, deliverance, and guidance (Psalm 37:18; 145:18).

Yahweh commits Himself to a particular people whom He chooses. His commitment flows purely out of a compassionate, gracious love in Himself and is not based on any merit of His people (Deuteronomy 7:6-9).

Yahweh's intention toward you is not simply an association, but an intimate union. He joins His life with yours. He gives Himself to you, and you belong to Him (see Isaiah 43:1).

The result of union with Yahweh is deliverance, power, resource for every need, comfort for every care, and His presence for every perplexity (Isaiah 43:2-3).

Yahweh is God's memorial name, used 6823 times in the Old Testament, reminding you that He is everything you need. He is your God. He is Creator. He is eternal. By virtue of His very existence, He is everything He has revealed Himself to be (Exodus 3:13-15; 34:5-7).

Yahweh keeps His promises. He is the authority and stands for truth—that which corresponds to reality. What Yahweh says, He will do (Deuteronomy 31:5-8; Joshua 21:45; Psalm 37:5).

Yahweh is eternal—the same yesterday, today, and forever (1 Chronicles 16:36; Psalm 72:18-19).

Yahweh is self-existent, the uncreated Creator. Everything else is created by Yahweh. He alone possesses the ability to make something out of nothing (Isaiah 40:28-31; 43:1,15).

Yahweh commits Himself to a people—He wants you (Jeremiah 31:31-34).

Yahweh makes a promise of deliverance (Psalm 18:1-2; Jeremiah 39:17-18).

Yahweh knows and sees all things, including the circumstances and hearts of His people (Exodus 3:7; 1 Samuel 16:7; Lamentations 3:50).

Yahweh never leaves those who are His (Isaiah 43:1-4).

Yahweh defends His people and protects His people (Psalm 27:1; 28:8).

Yahweh is jealous for the love of His people. He wants His people to love Him (Exodus 34:14, Deuteronomy 6:5; 30:20).

Yahweh acts with purpose toward His people (Isaiah 55:8-12; Jeremiah 29:11-13).

RECOMMENDED READING

Alexander, Myrna, and Ralph Alexander. *Behold Your God.* Grand Rapids: Zondervan, 1978.

Arthur, Kay. *Lord, I Want to Know You.* Colorado Springs: Waterbrook Press, 2000.

Bright, Bill. *God: Discover His Character.* Orlando: New Life Publications, 2002.

Charnock, Stephen. *The Existence and Attributes of God.* Grand Rapids: Baker Book House, 1979.

Eastman, Dick. *A Celebration of Praise.* Grand Rapids: Baker Book House, 1984.

Hemphill, Ken. *The Names of God.* Nashville: B&H, 2001.

Jukes, Andrew. *The Names of God.* Grand Rapids: Kregel, 1967.

Lockyer, Herbert. *All the Divine Names and Titles in the Bible.* Grand Rapids: Zondervan, 1975.

MacDonald, William. *Alone in Majesty.* Spring Lake: Christian Missions in Many Lands, 2004.

Packer, J.I. *Knowing God.* Downers Grove: InterVarsity Press, 1993.

Smith, Hanna Whitall. *The God of All Comfort.* Chicago: Moody Press, 1956.

Spangler, Ann. *Praying the Names of God.* Grand Rapids: Zondervan, 2004.

Stone, Nathan. *Names of God.* Chicago: Moody Press, 1944.

Sumrall, Lester. *The Names of God.* New Kensington: Whitaker House, 2006.

Towns, Elmer. *My Father's Names.* Ventura: Regal Books, 1991.

Tozer, A.W. *Men Who Met God.* Camp Hill: Christian Publications, 1986.

———. *The Knowledge of the Holy.* San Francisco: HarperCollins, 1992.

———. *The Pursuit of God.* Camp Hill: Christian Publications, 1993.

NOTES

INTRODUCTION

Epigraph. A.W. Tozer, *The Pursuit of God* (Camp Hill, PA: Christian Publications, 1993), p. 121.

1. Quoted in A.W. Tozer, *The Christian Book of Mystical Verse* (Camp Hill, PA: Christian Publications, 1963), pp. 12-14.

DAY 1

1. Charles Spurgeon, *Spurgeon's Sermons,* vol. 1 (Albany, NY: Ages Software, 1998).

DAY 2

1. Paul Enns, *The Moody Handbook of Theology,* (Chicago: Moody Press, 1989), p. 156.

2. Sheldon Vanauken, *A Severe Mercy* (San Francisco: Harper & Row, 1977), p. 93.

3. Enns, *The Moody Handbook of Theology,* p. 159.

4. Howard F. Vos, *Beginnings in the Old Testament* (Chicago: Moody Press, 1975), p. 23.

DAY 3

1. William Sanford La Sor, David Allan Hubbard, Frederic William Bush, *Old Testament Survey* (Grand Rapids: Eerdmans, 1982), p. 134.

2. Kenneth Barker, et al., eds., *Zondervan TNIV Study Bible* (Grand Rapids: Zondervan, 2006), p. 265.

3. Annie Johnson Flint, *Best-Loved Poems* (Toronto: Evangelical Publishers, n.d.), pp. 101-102.

DAY 4

1. Oswald Chambers, *My Utmost for His Highest* (Grand Rapids: Discovery House), July 4 and 5.

DAY 5

1. Hannah Whitall Smith, *The God of All Comfort* (Chicago: Moody Press, 1956), p. 234.

DAY 6

1. "My Master's Face," in Robert Parsons, comp., *Quotes from the Quiet Hour* (Chicago: Moody Press, 1949), p. 94.

DAY 7

1. For more study on God and His Word as the authority for your belief, see "The Truth About Truth" in my book *Knowing and Loving the Bible* (Eugene: Harvest House, 2007), pp. 77-83.

2. See *Knowing and Loving the Bible* for more detailed information on word studies.

3. Wesley L. Duewel, *Heroes of the Holy Life* (Grand Rapids: Zondervan, 2002), pp. 22-23.

DAY 8

1. I-Jin Loh and Howard Hatton, *A Handbook on the Letter from James,* UBS Handbook Series (New York: United Bible Societies, 1997), p. 149.

2. Howard F. Vos, *Beginnings in the Old Testament* (Chicago: Moody Press, 1975), p. 63.

3. A.W. Tozer, *The Pursuit of God,* (Camp Hill, PA: Christian Publications, 1993), p. 10.

4. A.W. Tozer, *The Knowledge of the Holy* (San Francisco: HarperCollins, 1992), p. 2.

5. Henri J.M. Nouwen, *The Way of the Heart* (New York: Ballantine Books, 1981), p. 9.

6. Josef Pieper, *Leisure, the Basis of Culture* (New York: Pantheon Books, 1963), pp. 40-42.

7. Don Postema, *Space for God* (Grand Rapids: CRC Publications, 1983), p. 15.

8. *Williams New Testament in the Language of the People.* Copyright © 1995, Charlotte Williams Sprawls. All rights reserved.

DAY 9

1. C.H. Spurgeon and Roy H. Clarke, *Beside Still Waters* (Nashville: Thomas Nelson, 2000), p. 87.

DAY 10

1. Spiros Zodhiates, *The Complete Word Study Old Testament* (Chattanooga: AMG, 1994), p. 2362.

2. R. Laird Harris, Gleason L. Archer Jr., and Bruce K. Waltke, *Theological Wordbook of the Old Testament,* vol. 2 (Chicago: Moody Press, 1980), p. 2063.

3. Jerry Bridges, *Trusting God* (Colorado Springs: NavPress, 1988), p. 18.

4. Octavius Winslow, *Help Heavenward* (Carlisle: The Banner of Truth Trust, 2000), p. 1.

5. For detailed discussion of how to find hope in the promises of God, read my book *Walking with the God Who Cares* (Eugene: Harvest House, 2007).

6. Annie Johnson Flint, *Best-Loved Poems* (Toronto: Evangelical Publishers, n.d.), p. 30.

DAY 11

1. Dick Eastman, *A Celebration of Praise* (Grand Rapids: Baker Book House, 1984), p. 17.

2. Darlene Zschech, *Extravagant Worship* (Minneapolis: Bethany House, 2002), pp. 59-60.

3. Zschech, *Extravagant Worship,* pp. 30-31.

4. From Augustine's exposition on Psalm 42.

DAY 12

1. Robert Parsons, comp., *Quotes from the Quiet Hour* (Chicago: Moody Press, 1949), p. 87.

2. Jerry Bridges, *Trusting God* (Colorado Springs: NavPress, 1988), p. 20.

DAY 13

1. R. Laird Harris, Gleason L. Archer Jr., and Bruce K. Waltke, *Theological Wordbook of the Old Testament,* vol. 1 (Chicago: Moody Press, 1980), pp. 39-40.

2. Henry M. Morris, *The Genesis Record* (Grand Rapids: Baker Book House, 1976), p. 39.

3. A.W. Tozer, *The Knowledge of the Holy* (San Francisco: HarperCollins, 1992), p. 30.

4. Herbert Lockyer, *All the Divine Names and Titles in the Bible* (Grand Rapids: Zondervan, 1975), p. 6.

5. Nathan Stone, *Names of God* (Chicago: Moody Press, 1944), p. 12.

6. Text by Civilla Martin, 1905.

DAY 14

1. Spiros Zodhiates, *The Complete Word Study Old Testament* (Chattanooga: AMG, 1994), p. 2349.

2. Henry M. Morris, *The Genesis Record* (Grand Rapids: Baker Book House, 1976), p. 318.

3. Herbert Lockyer, *All the Divine Names and Titles in the Bible* (Grand Rapids: Zondervan, 1975), p. 9.

DAY 15

1. Nathan Stone, *Names of God* (Chicago: Moody Press, 1944), p. 43.

2. Stone, *Names of God,* pp. 45-46.

3. Kenneth Barker, et al., eds., *Zondervan TNIV Study Bible* (Grand Rapids: Zondervan, 2006), p. 1898.

4. Catherine Martin, *Revive My Heart!* (Colorado Springs: NavPress, 2003). From the foreword by Bill Bright.

5. Quoted in Herbert Lockyer, *All the Divine Names and Titles in the Bible* (Grand Rapids: Zondervan, 1975), p. 16.

DAY 16

1. Spiros Zodhiates, *The Complete Word Study Old Testament* (Chattanooga: AMG, 1994), p. 2371.

2. Herbert Lockyer, *All the Divine Names and Titles in the Bible* (Grand Rapids: Zondervan, 1975), p. 14. See also Nathan Stone, *Names of God* (Chicago: Moody Press, 1944), p. 34.

3. Quoted in Lockyer, *All the Divine Names and Titles in the Bible,* p. 14.

4. Stephen Charnock, *The Existence and Attributes of God,* vol. 2 (Grand Rapids: Baker Book House, 1979), p. 13.

5. Hannah Whitall Smith, *The God of All Comfort* (Chicago: Moody Press, 1956), pp. 247-49.

6. Quoted in Courtney Anderson, *To the Golden Shore* (Grand Rapids: Zondervan, 1972), p. 499.

7. V. Raymond Edman, *The Disciplines of Life* (Chicago: Van Kampen Press, 1948), p. 25.

8. Edman, *The Disciplines of Life,* p. 245.

DAY 17

1. Herbert Lockyer, *All the Divine Names and Titles in the Bible* (Grand Rapids: Zondervan, 1975), p. 21.

2. Lockyer, *All the Divine Names and Titles in the Bible,* pp. 21-22.

3. Dwight Hervey Small, *No Rival Love,* (Fort Washington, PA: Christian Literature Crusade, 1984), p. 104.

4. A.W. Tozer, *Men Who Met God* (Camp Hill, PA: Christian Publications, 1986), p. 73.

5. Tozer, *Men Who Met God,* pp. 73-74.

DAY 18

1. F.B. Meyer, *Devotional Commentary* (Wheaton: Tyndale House, 1989), p. 18.

DAY 19

1. Gordon J. Wenham, *Word Biblical Commentary,* vol. 2, *Genesis 16–50* (Dallas: Word, 2002), p. 11.

2. William MacDonald, *Alone in Majesty* (Spring Lake: Christian Missions in Many Lands, 2004), p. 30.

DAY 20

1. Herbert Lockyer, *All the Divine Names and Titles in the Bible* (Grand Rapids: Zondervan, 1975), p. 17.

DAY 21

1. Nathan Stone, *Names of God* (Chicago: Moody Press, 1944), p. 72.

2. Adapted from Mrs. Charles Cowman, *Springs in the Valley* (Los Angeles: The Oriental Missionary Society, 1939), p. 358.

DAY 22

1. Nathan Stone, *Names of God* (Chicago: Moody Press, 1944), pp. 87-88.

2. Herbert Lockyer, *All the Divine Names and Titles in the Bible* (Grand Rapids: Zondervan, 1975), p. 31.

DAY 23

1. Nathan Stone, *Names of God* (Chicago: Moody Press, 1944), p. 97.

2. R.C. Sproul, *The Holiness of God* (Wheaton: Tyndale House, 1985), p. 54.

3. A.W. Tozer, *The Knowledge of the Holy* (San Francisco: HarperCollins, 1992), p. 165.

4. For more information on how to live in the power of the Holy Spirit, read my book *Set My Heart on Fire* (Eugene: Harvest House, 2007).

5. Dick Eastman, *A Celebration of Praise* (Grand Rapids: Baker Book House, 1984), p. 60.

DAY 24

1. Quoted in Mrs. Charles Cowman, *Springs in the Valley* (Los Angeles: The Oriental Missionary Society, 1939), pp. 349-50.

DAY 25

1. Herbert Lockyer, *All the Divine Names and Titles in the Bible* (Grand Rapids: Zondervan, 1975), p. 39.

2. Spiros Zodhiates, *The Complete Word Study New Testament* (Chattanooga: AMG, 1993).

3. Alan Redpath, *The Making of a Man of God* (Old Tappan, NJ: Revell, 1962), pp. 90,93.

4. Quoted in Mrs. Charles Cowman, *Springs in the Valley* (Los Angeles: The Oriental Missionary Society, 1939), p. 125.

DAY 26

1. Herbert Lockyer, *All the Divine Names and Titles in the Bible* (Grand Rapids: Zondervan, 1975), p. 44.

2. Quoted in Robert Parsons, comp., *Quotes from the Quiet Hour* (Chicago: Moody Press, 1949), p. 69.

DAY 27

1. Nathan Stone, *Names of God* (Chicago: Moody Press, 1944), p. 141.

DAY 28

1. Leon Morris, *The Epistle to the Romans* (Grand Rapids: Eerdmans, 1988), p. 315.

2. Cited in James Montgomery Boice, *Romans,* vol. 2, *The Reign of Grace* (Grand Rapids: Baker Book House, 1995), p. 842.

3. Elmer Towns, *My Father's Names* (Ventura: Regal Books, 1991), p. 152.

4. Herbert Lockyer, *All the Divine Names and Titles in the Bible* (Grand Rapids: Zondervan, 1975), p. 65.

5. A.W. Tozer, *The Knowledge of the Holy* (New York: Harper & Row, 1961), p. 105.

DAY 30

1. Alan Redpath, *The Making of a Man of God* (Old Tappan, NJ: Revell, 1962), pp. 13-14.

ACKNOWLEDGMENTS

No book is ever written without the assistance and encouragement of countless people.

I could have never written this book without the constant support and encouragement of my family. Thank you, David, my dear husband, for always reminding me of God's eternal perspective at just the right time. Thank you for your editing capabilities and creative direction in every book project. And thank you for loving me all these years of marriage. Rob, thank you for being the best brother a girl could ever have and for your early-morning phone calls. Mother, thank you for your constant prayers, steadfast love, and words of assurance. You are my great example in life. Dad, you are one of my heroes and always say just the right thing to keep me running my race. And Eloise, Andy, Keegan, James, Tania, Christopher, and Kayla—I'm so thankful for you—you are bright, shining stars in my life.

Thank you to my dear friends—Andy Graybill, Beverly Trupp, Cindy Clark, Conni Hudson, Shirley Peters, Kelly Abeyratne, Julie Airis, Helen Peck, Stefanie Kelly, Carolyn Haynes, Myra Murphy, Lou Major, Judy Lorenz, John and Betty Mann, Paula Zillmer, Kayla Branscum, Vonette Bright, and Josh and Dottie McDowell.

Thank you to my assistant at Quiet Time Ministries, Kayla Branscum, who handles myriads of responsibilities with ease and keeps everything going at our Quiet Time Ministries Resource and Training Center. Thank you, Charlie Branscum, for your help in a thousand ways in Quiet Time Ministries. Thank you also to Paula Zillmer for your faithful contribution to our ministry. Thank you to the Quiet Time Ministries team, the board of directors, the *Enriching Your Quiet Time* magazine staff, and those who partner financially and prayerfully with Quiet Time Ministries. A special thank you to all those who piloted *Trusting in the Names of God*—your insights and comments were invaluable to the final result of this book.

Thank you to Shelley Smith, our Women's Ministries assistant at Southwest Community Church, for helping me and serving our women. Thank you to the women at SCC for your love and support and to the staff at Southwest.

Thank you to Dr. Ronald Youngblood, one of the translators of the NIV and TNIV, for your insight into the names of God and the Dead Sea Scrolls, for your invaluable help with English transliterations and areas specific to the original languages, and for your encouragement of me in ministry since the days when I studied with great joy and excitement in your Old Testament classes in seminary.

My friend, Pastor Jim Smoke—thank you for your constant encouragement as I write. I still am amazed that the Lord brought you to the desert, and so thankful! Greg Johnson, my agent—thank you for loving the Lord, believing in me, and encouraging me to write books. And thank you to Bob Hawkins Sr.—I will forever look back on the day I met you as so amazing and will never forget the twinkle in your eye as you shook my hand and talked with me about books. Your passion and excitement for publishing books is totally contagious!

I am thankful for Harvest House Publishers, who encourages me to dream big. You make writing books so much fun. I'd like to thank the entire Harvest House team, including LaRae Weikert, Steve Miller, John Constance, Barb Sherrill, Katie Lane, Betty Fletcher, Jeana Newman, Christianne Debysingh, Shane White, Rob Teigen, Dave Bartlett, Lisa Birkby, Abby Van Wormer, Elizabeth Colclough, Peggy Wright, and Kimberly Shumate. A special thanks to Terry Glaspey for your vision and your encouragement of me in writing the books God has called me to write. And then, a huge thank you to Gene Skinner for editing my books with such impeccable detail, discernment, and dedication to the Lord. And finally, thank you to Bob Hawkins Jr., president of Harvest House, for loving the Lord, for encouraging me as I write the books God has placed on my heart, and for your incredible leadership of one of the best teams on the planet. You have been such an example for me as I lead others in Quiet Time Ministries.

Thank you to Joni Eareckson Tada for giving me Acts 20:24 at the outset of the writing of this book. I held on to those words for strength, comfort, encouragement, and endurance throughout the journey.

Finally, to the Lord—I want to say thank You for being my constant comfort, joy, strength, hope, and steadfast champion. I can't wait to see You face-to-face when I step from time into eternity. Until then, may I be faithful to discover, draw near to, declare, depend on, and delight in You. May I, day by day, trust in Your names.

ABOUT THE AUTHOR

Catherine Martin is a summa cum laude graduate of Bethel Theological Seminary with a master of arts degree in theological studies. She is founder of Quiet Time Ministries, a director of women's ministries, and a member of the adjunct faculty of Biola University. Teaching at retreats and conferences, she challenges others to seek God and love Him with all of their heart, soul, mind, and strength.

About Quiet Time Ministries

Quiet Time Ministries teaches devotion to God and Word to men and women throughout the world. Contact us for more information.

Quiet Time Ministries
PO Box 14007
Palm Desert, CA 92255
1-800-925-6458
www.quiettime.org

AVAILABLE FROM
QUIET TIME MINISTRIES

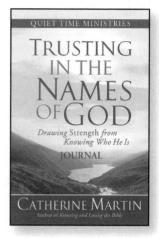

Trusting in the Names of God Journal

This companion journal is designed for use with your 30-day journey of *Trusting in the Names of God*. It includes journal and prayer pages taken from the *Quiet Time Notebook*, published by Quiet Time Ministries Press.

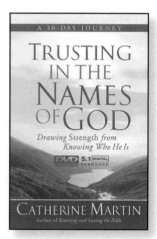

Trusting in the Names of God DVD

This professionally filmed, two-DVD set includes six 30-minute messages from Catherine Martin. These engaging presentations—an introductory message and one message for each week of the 30-day journey *Trusting in the Names of God*—are perfect for personal use or for groups.

Other Great Harvest House Books by Catherine Martin

TRUSTING IN THE NAMES OF GOD— A QUIET TIME EXPERIENCE

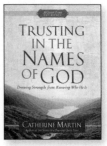

This full-length companion volume is more than a study guide—it is filled with eight weeks of actual quiet times. It includes devotional readings, Bible studies, hymns, journaling opportunities, prayers, and practical applications—everything you need to be inspired, to be encouraged, and to gain the most from your quiet time experiences.

SIX SECRETS TO A POWERFUL QUIET TIME

Are you enjoying the closeness with God you desire? Are your prayer times transforming your life from the inside out? Are you sensing God speaking to you through your Bible reading? Now you can join Catherine Martin on an exciting 30-day journey to discover how to really have a quiet time.

KNOWING AND LOVING THE BIBLE

This powerful, interactive 30-day journey transforms reading and studying the Bible into acts of love and brings you closer to God as you discover nourishment for daily living and build a foundation on His promises.

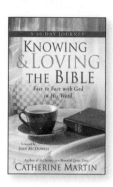

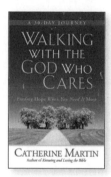

WALKING WITH THE GOD WHO CARES

Catherine Martin demonstrates how to experience a deep and abiding sense of joy in the midst of sorrow and pain: through an intimate relationship with the God who cares and a complete dependence on His Word. This 30-day journey is packed with inspiring stories, powerful promises, stimulating quiet time plans, and more.

SET MY HEART ON FIRE

If you long for a personal revival, you will find all you need in this 30-day journey. This passionate invitation uses biblical teaching, inspirational stories, and personal anecdotes to gently but effectively lead you into a deeper walk with the Lord.

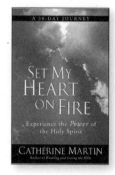